ROME
nan MapGuides

Welcome to Rome!

This opening fold-out contains a general map of Rome to help you visualise the large districts discussed in this guide, and four pages of valuable information, handy tips and useful addresses.

Discover Rome through six districts and six maps

A Campo dei Fiori / Pantheon / Piazza Navona
B Vaticano / Piazza Cavour / Prati
C Testaccio / Aventino / Trastevere / Ghetto
D Tridente / Piazza del Popolo / Villa Borghese
E Quirinale / Esquilino / Termini
F Caracalla / San Giovanni / Colosseo

For each district there is a double-page of addresses (restaurants – listed in ascending order of price – cafés, bars, tearooms, music venues and shops), followed by a fold-out map for the relevant area with the essential places to see (indicated on the map by a star ★). These places are by no means all that Rome has to offer, but to us they are unmissable. The grid-referencing system (**A** B2) makes it easy for you to pinpoint addresses quickly on the map.

Transportation and hotels in Rome

The last fold-out consists of a transport map and four pages of practical information that include a selection of hotels.

Index

Lists all the street names, monuments and places to visit featured in this guide.

DISTRICTS

Since 1921 the city has been divided into 22 *rioni* (districts) – Monti, Trastevere, Testaccio... The map (left) shows the main landmarks, the city's hills (Quirinale, Esquilino) and other place names such as Il Tridente (so-called due to the shape formed by the three main roads spreading out from Piazza del Popolo).

VATICAN CITY

Since 1929, it has had its own currency, diplomats and postal system, which is faster than the regular Italian mail (blue boxes).

RIONE MONTI

ARTS

Antiquity
Under Imperial Rome (27 BC–AD 476), stadia, acqueducts, thermal baths, temples and mausoleums were all built with the same material: freestone and brick adorned with marble. From the 2nd century, cement appeared for use in arches, vaults and monumental cupolas. Three styles evolved: Tuscan (smooth shaft, plain capital), Doric Roman (fluted shaft, molded capital) and composite (capital decorated with a volute and acanthus): **Pantheon** (**A** D3).

Renaissance and Mannerism (15th–16th c.)
A universal revival, caught up in the humanist trend of the period. The ideas of antiquity – updated by the tastes of the period – and the influence of science, resulted in an art centred on Man. Symmetry and a sense of proportion were key to all creative works: **Bramante** (1444–1514); **Peruzzi** (1481–1536).

Baroque (17th–18th c.) Aiming to inspire the masses, Baroque art, with Rome as its founder and Il Bernini (1598–1680) as its master, developed a taste for splendor. Architects and designers (Da Cortona: 1596–1669, Borromini: 1599–1667) created curves, counter-curves and optical illusions, and used various materials in the same work (bronze and colored marbles): **Trevi fountain** (**E** A2).

Cineporto
→ *Tel. 06 36 08 53 33*
Stadio Olimpico park. Two films per evening on each of the two screens (July-Aug).
Cinema Nuovo Sacher (**C** C4)
→ *Largo Ascianghi*
Films in the open air (Aug).
Madonna della Neve
Shower of white flowers at Sta Maria Maggiore (Aug 5).
December
Immaculate Conception Festival of the Virgin Mary, Piazza di Spagna (Dec 8).
Christmas All churches hold midnight mass (Dec 24); papal blessing (Dec 25).

OPENING HOURS

Churches
Usually daily 8am–12.30pm, 4–7pm.
Green spaces
Dawn until dusk.
Museums
Usually Tue-Sun 9am–7pm. Last admission one hour before closing time.

Restaurants
Mon-Sat noon–3pm, 7.30–11pm. Restaurants are often closed on Mon and in Aug.
Shopping
Mon-Fri 10am–1pm, 3–7.30pm (or 8pm). Most close on Sun, Mon morning and in Aug.
Markets
Mon-Sat 7am–1pm.

EATING OUT

Trattorie or *osterie* are informal restaurants serving good, local, home-cooked Italian food.
Ristoranti tend to be more expensive and offer a large array of fancier dishes.
Enoteca: wine bar-restaurant.
Pizzeria: for a cheap yet often very good pizza.
Cover charge
Some restaurants add a cover charge that includes bread *(pane e coperto)* – usually €1–2 per person

(the price must be indicated on the menu) – as well as a service charge (10%).
The menu
Antipasti are starters (grilled vegetables, cold meats and cheeses), followed by *primi piatti* (pasta or risotto); the main course, or *secondi piatti* (meat or fish), is followed by cheese or *dolce* (dessert).
Fast food
Pizza al taglio are slices of pizza, sold by weight. *Bombe* (donuts), *cornetti* (croissants), *tramezzini* and *panini* (small white bread sandwiches) are sold in bars or on street corners.

GUIDED TOURS

Bus tours (**E** F2)
110 City Tour Open
→ *Daily 9am–8pm. Depart from Stazione Termini every 20 mins; €13*
Two-hour tours of Rome's most famous monuments.

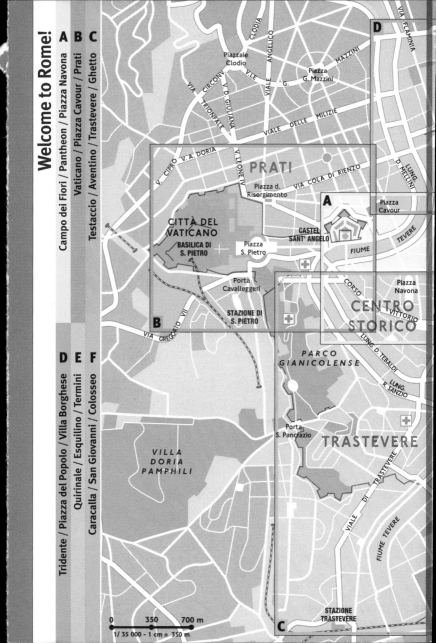

Welcome to Rome!

A Campo dei Fiori / Pantheon / Piazza Navona

B Vaticano / Piazza Cavour / Prati

C Testaccio / Aventino / Trastevere / Ghetto

D Tridente / Piazza del Popolo / Villa Borghese

E Quirinale / Esquilino / Termini

F Caracalla / San Giovanni / Colosseo

Piazzale
Clodio

Piazza
G. Mazzini

VIA FLAMINIA

VIA CLODIA

VIALE ANGELICO

VLE G. MAZZINI

VIA TRIONFALE

VIA CIRCONV. TRIONFALE

V. D. GIULIANA

VIALE DELLE MILIZIE

V. CIPRO   V. A. DORIA

V. LEONE IV

PRATI

Piazza d.
Risorgimento

VIA COLA DI RIENZO

LUNG. D. MELLINI

D

A

Piazza
Cavour

**CITTÀ DEL
VATICANO**

**BASILICA DI
S. PIETRO**

Piazza
S. Pietro

**CASTEL
SANT' ANGELO**

FIUME   TEVERE

Porta
Cavalleggeri

CORSO VITTORIO

Piazza
Navona

**CENTRO
STORICO**

B

**STAZIONE DI
S. PIETRO**

VIA GREGORIO VII

LUNG. D. TEBALDI

LUNG.
R. SANZIO

**PARCO
GIANICOLENSE**

Porta
S. Pancrazio

TRASTEVERE

**VILLA
DORIA
PAMPHILI**

VIALE DI TRASTEVERE

FIUME TEVERE

**STAZIONE
TRASTEVERE**

C

0   350   700 m

1/ 35 000 - 1 cm = 350 m

PIAZZA NAVONA

LANDMARKS

CITY PROFILE

- Capital of Italy
- 579 square miles
- 2.8 million inhabitants
- 14.5 million visitors each year
- 400 churches
- One river (the Tiber)
- Currency: the euro (€)

WWW

→ *romaturismo.com*
The official Roman tourist office website.
→ *vatican.va*
The Vatican website.
→ *beniculturali.it*
The Ministry of Cultural Heritage website.
→ *enit.it*
The Italian Government Tourist Board website.
→ *roma-o-matic.com*
→ *romecity.it*
Practical and cultural information websites.

Cybercafés
Internet train
→ *Via dei Marrucini, 12*
Tel. 06 44 54 953
Mon-Fri 9.30am–1am;
Sat 5pm–1am

USEFUL INFO

PIT (Punti informativi turistici del comune di Roma)
→ *Tel. 06 82 05 91 27*

Information service for the Rome area: eight green kiosks throughout the city, with a telephone service in five languages.

Telephone codes
UK / USA to Italy
→ *Dial 00 (UK) / 011 (USA) + 39 (Italy) + 06 (Rome code with initial 0) + number*
Italy to UK / USA
→ *Dial 00 + 44 (UK) / 1 (USA) + number without initial 0 for UK numbers*
Within Italy
→ *Dial the city code (incl. the initial 0) + number*

Useful telephone numbers
Carabinieri (police): *112*
Ambulance service: *118*
Fire service: *115*
US Embassy
→ *Via Vittorio Veneto 119/A*
Tel. 06 46741 (switchboard)
www.usembassy.it
UK Embassy
→ *Via XX Settembre 80*
Tel 06 4220 0001 (out of office hours 06 4220 2603)

DIARY OF EVENTS

March
San Giuseppe: Donuts and pancakes in the Trionfale district (March 19).
April
Santa Semana: Stations of the Cross, from the Coliseum to the Palentine (Good Friday). At noon on Easter Sunday, papal blessing: Piazza San Pietro.
June
San Giovanni: Traditional snail-tasting (June 23). Sung mass at San Giovanni in Laterano (June 24).
San Pietro e san Paolo Sung mass at San Pietro (June 29).
July-August
Numerous events. Information available from the commune of Rome.
→ *Tel. 06 06 06*
www.estateromana.comune. roma.it
Concerti nel parco
Open-air concerts in Villa

Pamphilj, in Pincio park
(**D** C3) or in the cloister of Trinità dei Monti (**D** D4) (end June-end July).
Fiesta!
→ *Via Appia Nuova, 1245*
Tel. 06 718 21 39
Latin music festival on the racetrack at Campanelle (June-Aug).
Teatro dell'Opera (F C4)
→ *Tel. 06 48 16 01*
Reservations: Tue-Sat 10am–4pm; Sun 9am–1.30pm
Opera at the Terme di Caracalla (July-Aug).
Jazz and image (F C3)
→ *Villa Celimontana*
Tel. 06 39 75 18 77
Club Alexanderplatz moves to the park at Villa Celimontana: jazz concerts, film screenings (June-Aug).
All'ombra del Colosseo
→ *Viale della Civiltà del Lavoro. Tel. 06 709 6281*
Cabaret and concerts in the EUR neighborhood (end June-beg Aug).

Piazza Navona is built on the site of Rome's first stadium, the Domitian. It is an elegant square, and retains the stadium's oblong shape. At the center of this lively, terrace-lined piazza stands the Fontana dei Quattro Fiumi (the 'fountain of four rivers'). Walk around the quiet back streets to the west of the square: Via della Pace, Via del Fico – looking up you may catch a glimpse of a hanging garden. To the east, the gigantic Pantheon seems tucked away in a tiny piazza. In the evening, once the sightseers have gone, the area regains its state of calm as, further south, Campo dei Fiori springs into life: the perfect place for an early or a late-night drink.

DA BAFFETTO   DAR FILETTARO

RESTAURANTS, PIZZERIAS

Da Baffetto (**A** B3)
→ Via del Governo Vecchio, 114 Tel. 06 686 16 17
Daily 6.30pm–1am.
Da Baffetto 2 (**A** C4): Piazza del Teatro di Pompeo, 18.
Daily noon–3pm, 6pm–1am
Terrific pizzeria making pizzas with deliciously thin, light and crispy crusts (the mozzarella and prosciutto one is a favorite). Eat in the sunny or shady parts of the large, pretty terrace. Always busy, so try to go very early or very late.
Pizza €4.50–10.
Dar Filettaro a Santa Barbara (**A** C4)
→ Largo dei Librari, 88
Tel. 06 686 40 18
Mon-Sat 5.30–11.10pm
Tiny restaurant close to Campo dei Fiori, in a small square beside a little church. Ten outdoor tables. Try the fried baccalà (cod), as nobody does it better in the city.
À la carte €15.
Da Alfredo e Ada (**A** B3)
→ Via dei Banchi Nuovi, 14
Tel. 06 687 88 42
Mon-Fri 1–4pm, 8–10pm
There's no sign or logo to catch your eye, just a dining room opening onto the street. There is no

menu either, it is the grandmotherly Ada who decides. As soon as you sit down she will serve you with a jug of vino bianco della casa (house white wine), then pasta, followed by a main course: involtini di vitello (stuffed veal escalope), or homemade sausages with lentils or beans (salsiccia con fagioli). Regulars tend to talk loudly, laugh a lot and even help themselves from the fridge. Allow for around €18 including wine (but the bill depends on how much Ada likes you).
Quelli della Taverna(**A** D4)
→ Via dei Barbieri, 25
Tel. 06 686 96 60
Tue-Sun 8.30pm–midnight
In a small street off Largo Argentina, a traditional taverna with seating at large tables. Generous helpings of antipasti misti (cheese, cold meats, grilled vegetables) and fresh pasta al dente (the one with cep mushrooms and truffles is divine).
À la carte €25.
L'Orso' 80 (**A** C2)
→ Via dell' Orso, 33
Tel. 06 686 49 04 Tue-Sun 1–3.30pm, 7.30–11.30pm
A glance at the extra-ordinary antipasti buffet tells you that L'Orso'80

3

2

1

S. AGNESE IN AGONE

PIAZZA NAVONA

S. MARIA D. ANIMA

PAL. DI GOVERNO VECCHIO

PAL. D. GOVERNO VECCHIO

CHIESA NUOVA

PAL. SFORZA CESARINI

VIA DEI CESARINI

VIA D. CORALLO

d. Orologio

Piazza d'Fico

CORSO VITTORIO

VIA SUGARELLI

VIA DI

PALAZZO SACCHETTI

VIA DI PARIONE

VIA DI TOR MILLINA

VIA D. TEATRO PACE

VIA DELLA PACE

VIA DI M.TE GIORDANO

VIA DI BANCHI NUOVI

Largo Tassoni

LUNGOTEVERE D.

VIA GIULIA

VIA D. FIORENTINI

VIA ACCIAIOLI

Largo Febo

Pia Cinqu

S. MARIA D. PACE

VIE DELLE VETRINA VACCHE

PALAZZO TAVERNA

VIA PAOLA

FIORENTINI

VIA DI PANICO

Piazza Sanguigna

VIA DEI CORONARI

V. DE' BANCO DI S. SPIRITO

Piazza P. Paoli

MUSEO NAZ ROMAN

Piazza

V. DEI TRE ARCHI

VIA MASCHERA D'ORELLI

PAL. LANCELLOTTI

S. SALVATORE IN LAURO

Piazza del Coronari

S. Salvatore in Lauro

PALAZ ALTEM

VIA ZANARD

D'ACQUA SPARTA

LUNGOTEVERE TOR DI NONA

ALTOVITI

LUNG. D. ALTOVITI

Piazza Pte S. Angelo

LUNG. D. VITTORIO EMANUELE II

VIA DELL

LUNG. DI MC

Piazza Umberto I Ponte

PONTE UMBERTO I

FIUME

PONTE S. ANGELO

PONTE S. ANGELO

LUNG. VATICANO

LUNG. DI

LUNG. PE

TEVERE

FIUME

Ponte Umberto I

LUNGOTEVERE CASTELLO

Pia Pia

Largo Mutilati ed Invalidi di Guerra

MAUSOLEO DI ADRIANO

Piazza dei Tribunali

CASA MADRE DEI MUTILATI

VIA TRIBONIANO

PALAZZO DI GIUSTIZIA

SACRO CUORE D. SUFFRAGIO

VIA P. MERCURI

VIA ULPIANO

CASTEL SANT'ANGELO

PIAZZA ADRIANA

PIAZZA ADRIANA

VIA P. DELLA VALLE

VIA ALBERICO II

C

VIA V. COLONN

VIA M. CLEMENTI

VIA P. DIONIGI

VIA CAVALLINI

VIA G. DA PALESTRINA

VIA CALAMATTA

Piazza Cavour

PIAZZA ADRIANA

VIA CRESCENZIO

B

TEATRO ADRIANO

VIA TACITO

VIA VIRGILIO

VIA ORAZIO

VIA CRESCENZIO

VIA OVIDIO

A

PALAZZO ALTEMPS

SANTA MARIA DELLA PACE

CHIESA NUOVA

SAN LUIGI DEI FRANCESI

PANTHEON

SANTA MARIA SOPRA MINE

★ **Chiesa Nuova** (**A** B3)
→ *Piazza della Chiesa Nuova*
Tel. 06 687 52 89 Daily
7.45am–noon, 4.30–7.30pm
Counter-Reformation
priest and founder of the
Oratorian Confederation,
Philip Neri commissioned
the building of the Chiesa
Nuova in 1575. Frescos by
Pietro da Cortona and
Baroccio (1533–1612); three
masterpieces by Rubens,
amongst which is *Burial of
Christ,* after Caravaggio.
The Baroque splendor of
the building is in complete
contrast to the simplicity
intended by its founder. To
the right of the church is the
Oratorio dei Filippini, by
Borromini, where concerts

have been performed
since the 1600s.
★ **Palazzo Altemps** (**A** C2)
→ *Piazza di Sant'Apollinare*
Tel. 06 39 96 77 00
Tue–Sun 9am–7.45pm
This 15th-century palace
now houses sculpture from
the National Roman
Museum (see **E**): Greek
originals (*Ludovisi's Throne,*
5th century BC) and some
remarkable Roman copies.
★ **Santa Maria
della Pace** (**A** C3)
→ *Via della Pace, 5*
Mon–Fri 10am–noon
A stunning example of
Baroque design. In 1656
Pietro da Cortona rebuilt the
square and, in a subtle
play of curves, incorporated

the church (first built in the
15th century) into his plan.
Don't miss Raphael's fresco,
Sibyls, in the Chigi chapel;
the Ponzetti chapel with
frescos by Baltassare
Peruzzi; and the cloister
(c.1500), the first in Rome
to be built by Bramante.
★ **Piazza Navona** (**A** C3)
This piazza is built on the
site of Domitian's stadium
(1st century AD). In the 17th
century, soon after being
elected, Innocent X decided
to embellish the square in
honor of his family, the
Pamphilj. Borromini rebuilt
the palace and the church
of Sant'Agnese in Agone,
and Bernini designed the
enormous Fontana dei

Fiumi (1651). The comb
genius of these master
makes this piazza a tru
Baroque masterpiece.
★ **Sant'Agostino** (**A**
→ *Via della Scrofa, 80*
Tel. 06 68 80 19 62
Daily 8am–noon, 4–7.30
A must-see for its two
masterpieces: Raphae
fresco, *The Prophet Isa*
(1512), and Caravaggio
Madonna of the Pilgrir
(1603–5).
★ **San Luigi
dei Francesi** (**A** D3)
→ *Piazza San Luigi dei
Francesi, 20. Tel. 06 688*
Daily (except Thu afterno
8.30am–12.30pm, 3.30–
In the Contarelli chape
The Calling of St Matth

IAZZA DEL CAMPIDOGLIO (CAPITOL)

PAINTERS

Michelangelo (1475–1564)
Seen as the embodiment of the Renaissance. His representation of human anatomy was to revolutionize painting and sculpture. He had a great influence on his contemporaries.

Raphael (1483–1520)
Bringing the Renaissance to its apogée, Raphael's work concerned order, precision and the harmony of drawing and color.

Caravaggio (1571–1610)
The master of chiaroscuro, the contrast between light and dark. His work is marked by strong dramatic tension.

---

udio commentaries vailable in English.

rcheobus
→ Daily 9.30am–5.30pm (Oct-March, daily 9.45am–4pm).
eparts from Stazione Termini very hour; €8
he Via Appia Antica.

inea delle basiliche
→ Daily 8.30am–7.30pm.
eparts from Stazione Termini very 30 mins; €13
he major basilicas.

River Tiber cruises
ittle known – but a great vay to discover the river.

iber II (A C2)
→ Ponte Umberto 1
el. 06 446 3481
ue-Sun 11am–4.30pm;
uration 1 hr 45 mins; €15
onte Umberto I –
onte Duca d'Aosta.
→ Wed, Fri-Sun 8pm–midnight
March-Dec); €52 (dinner incl.)
rips along the Tiber, as far s Ponte Milvio and return.

attelli di Roma (B F3)
→ Ponte San Angelo
el. 06 68 30 15 85

Daily 12.30pm, 6pm, 5.30pm; duration 1 hr 15 mins; €12
Trip departing from Castel Sant'Angelo and return.
→ Thu-Sat 9pm; duration 2 hrs; €53 (incl. dinner)

Archeological sites
Advance reservation a must. Write to the commune of Rome (www.comune.roma.it)
In town
→ Tel. 06 67 10 38 19
Monte Testaccio, Teatro di Marcello, Mausoleo di Augusto, Area Sacra...
Outside town
→ Tel. 06 78 01 324
Churches
Most churches are free, but do bring some small change for lighting candles.
Dress code
Midriff, shoulders and thighs must be covered.
Museums
Reduced price tickets
■ Roma Archeologia Card
→ €20 for seven days
For four sections of the Museo Nazionale Romano

(National Roman Museum):
Palazzo Altemps, Palazzo Massimo, Cripta Balbi, Terme di Diocleziano; and for the Colosseo, Palatino, Terme di Caracalla, Tomba di Cecilia Metella and Villa dei Quintili.
■ Combined ticket
→ €7 for three days
Palazzo Altemps, Palazzo Massimo alle terme, Terme di Diocleziano, Cripta Balbi.
Free admission
Available to Europeans under 18 or over 65.
Settimana dei Beni Culturali
→ one week between end March and early May
Free entrance to all museums and monuments, and opening of some sites usually closed to the public.

CONCERTS, SHOWS

Concerts in churches
Most Sundays. Listings available from tourist offices.
Sung masses
San Giovanni in Laterano

(June 24); San Pietro (June 29); Gesù (Dec 31).
Auditorium Parco della musica
→ Viale Pietro De Coubertin
Mon-Fri by appt;
Sat-Sun 11.30am–4.30pm
Tel. 06 80 24 12 81
Entry €9
Concerts: tel. 06 80 24 23 50/1
www.auditoriumroma.com
Inaugurated in 2002, this complex, built and conceived by the architect Renzo Piano, comprises three auditoria and an arena for open-air shows, holding up to 3,000 people. Very eclectic program.
Ticket services
Orbis (E D3)
→ Piazza dell'Esquilino, 37
Tel. 06 474 47 76
Feltrinelli (B D1)
→ Viale Giulio Cesare, 88
Music store selling tickets.
Vivaticket
→ www.vivaticket.it
Tickets for shows, opera, concerts, festivals etc.

FOUNTAINS

Fontana di Trevi (E A2)
The most famous:
two Tritons guiding
two seahorses
toward the ocean.
**Fontana
del Tritone (E** B1)
By Bernini, on Piazza
Barberini: a huge Triton
blows into a conch shell.
**Fontana dei Quatro
Fiumi (A** C3)
The most famous of
Bernini's works: an
allegory of the rivers
of the four continents.
**Fontana
delle Tartarughe (C** D2)
The most charming:
four Adonises holding
tortoises.

EXCURSIONS

AROUND ROME

Centrale Montemartini
→ *Via Ostiense, 106*
Subway: Piramide
Tel. 06 574 8038
Tue-Sun 9.30am–7pm
Ancient sculptures in
a former power station.
EUR
→ *Subway: EUR*
Mussolini's monumental
Rome.
Via Appia Antica
→ *Bus no. 218 (Piazza San
Giovanni Laterano) or 118*
The Roman way.
**Catacombe
di San Callisto**
→ *Tel. 06 513 015 80*
Thu-Tue 9am–noon, 2–
5pm (5.30pm in summer).
Closed Feb
More than 12 miles of
burial chambers.
**Catacombe
di San Sebastiano**
→ *Tel. 06 788 03 50*
Mon-Sat 9am–noon,
2–5pm. Closed mid-Nov-
mid-Dec
First Christian burial site.
Ostia Antica
→ *Viale dei Romagnoli 717*
Tel. 06 563 580 99 Subway:
EUR then train (30 mins).
Tue-Sun 9am–5pm (7pm
in summer)
Remarkable remains of
an ancient Roman port.
Tivoli
→ *Subway: Ponte*
Mammolo then COTRAL
bus (30 mins)
Villa Adriana
→ *Tel. 07 74 53 0203*
Daily 9am–6pm
The magnificent Hadrian's
Villa, a genuine open-air
museum.
Villa d'Este
→ *Tel. 07 74 31 20 70*
Tue-Sun 8.30am–6.30pm
Incredible Italian-style
gardens: 500 fountains.

Reduced ticket prices
Theater, concerts
No reductions when buying
at the theater box office,
and you will be asked for
a 10% deposit. Reserve
months ahead for the
Teatro dell' Opera.
Cinema
Reduced-price tickets for
all shows, all day Wed.
Listings information
TrovaRoma
→ *Thursday*
Weekly supplement to the
Repubblica (culture, films).
Roma c'è
→ *Wednesday, €1.20*
Complete listings on
shows, theater, movies etc.

SHOPPING

Sales
Twice a year, at the
beginning of Jan and July.
Department stores
La Rinascente **(A** F2)
→ *Largo Chigi, 20*
Tel. 06 679 7691

Mon-Sat 10am–10pm;
Sun 10.30am–8pm
Italy's first department
store, opened in 1887.
Coin (F F3)
→ *Piazzale Appio, 7*
Tel. 06 708 00 20
Mon-Sat 9.30am–8pm;
Sun 10am–8pm
Shopping mall
Galleria Colonna-
Alberto Sordi **(A** F2)
→ *Piazza Colonna, 31-35*
Daily 10am–10pm
Magnificent Art Nouveau
gallery (1922). Clothing
and accessories.

GOING OUT

Campo dei Fiori (A C4)
Lovely square in the
centro storico (historic
center), lively until late.
Trastevere (C C3)
Bars, popular *osterie*
around Santa Maria.
San Lorenzo
Student district, to
the east of the Termini.

Monte Testaccio (C C5)
Favorite haunt for night
owls: bars, restaurants,
discos and the Villagio
Globale, the most revered
of the *centri sociali*.

GREEN SPACES

Parks and gardens
Villa Borghese **(D** D2)
A park with a 6-mile
circumference; gardens, a
wood, a lake, hippodrome,
museums and lawns.
Villa Doria Pamphilj
→ *Via di San Pancrazio /*
Via Aurelia Antica
Behind the Janiculum, the
largest public park in Rome.
Orto Botanico **(C** B2)
→ *Largo Cristina di Svezia, 24*
Tel. 06 49 91 7107
Tue-Sun 9.30am–6.30pm
(5.30pm in winter)
Entrance fee €4
Situated in the former
gardens of Villa Corsini:
7,000 types of plants
and a splendid waterfall.

STORICO

S. EUSTACHIO · S. IVO · VIA MONTERONE · SEDIARI · TEATRO VALLE · VITTORIO · VIA D. SUDARIO · TEATRO ARGENTINA · VIA D. FARINA · VIA D. BARBIERI · DEI MONTE DELLA FARINA · S. CARLO AI CATINARI · ARENULA · Largo Arenula

VIA TORRE ARGENTINA · V. ARCO DI CIAMBELLA · VIA DEI CESTARI · Largo Torre Argentina · EMANUELE II · AREA SACRA D. ARGENTINA · VIA ARCO DE' GINNASI

Piazza d. Minerva · ★ S. MARIA SOPRA MINERVA · Piazza d. Pigna · SS. STIMMATE DI S. FRANCESCO · VIA DEL GESÙ · VIA S. STEFANO DEL CACCO · Piazza del Gesù · ★ CHIESA DEL GESÙ · D'ASTALLI · V. D. BOTTEGHE OSCURE · PALAZZO MATTEI · Piazza Margana

V. D. ANGELICO · COLLEGIO ROMANO · Piazza Collegio Romano · PAL. DORIA PAMPHILI (GALLERIA) · Piazza Grazioli · VIA D. PLEBISCITO · D'ARACOELI · Piazza d'Aracoeli

S. MARIA IN VIA LATA · APOSTOLI · SS. APOSTOLI · Piazza SS. Apostoli · VIC. DE PIOMBO · VIA C. BATTISTI · S. MARCO · PAL. VENEZIA · Piazza Venezia · Piazza S. Marco · VIA S. MARCO · MON. A VITTORIO EMANUELE II · ALTARE DELLA PATRIA

CORSO · VIA D. CORSO · PALAZZO COLONNA (GALLERIA) · PALAZZO VALENTINI · Piazza Venezia · Piazza Madonna di Loreto

D · E · F · 4

CHIESA DEL GESÙ

PALAZZO FARNESE

atthew and the Angel The Martyrdom of atthew, all masterpieces aravaggio. They are early nples of his chiaroscuro nique, filled with erful, dramatic tension.

antheon (A D3)
→ azza della Rotonda
6 68 30 02 30
Sat 8.30am–7.30pm;
3.30am–1pm
best preserved of the ent Roman buildings .18–125). The cupola, ed with one single ication of cement over oden frame, is one of argest masonry domes built. The portico s onto a perfectly ortioned rotunda: five

concentric circles of coffers leading to the oculus, 30 ft in diameter and the only source of light in the temple. Kings Victor-Emmanuel II (1820–78) and Umberto I (1844–1900), and the artist Raphael are buried here.

★ Santa Maria sopra Minerva (A E3)
→ Piazza della Minerva, 42
Tel. 06 679 39 26
Mon-Sat 9am–noon, 4–6pm;
Sun 9am–4pm
A Christ by Michelangelo, frescos by Filippino Lippi (1457–1504) and the tombstone of Fra Angelico (1400–1455) create a rich decor in the only Gothic church in Rome, rebuilt in 1208 on the site of a temple

dedicated to Minerva. In front of the church stands an obelisk (6th century) supported by a small elephant, a curious mixture of images designed by Bernini and built by Ercole Ferrara in the 17th century.

★ Chiesa del Gesù (A E4)
→ Piazza del Gesù. Daily
6.45am–12.45pm, 4–7.45pm
The first Jesuit church (1568–73), it influenced Italian and European religious architecture for almost a century. The sober decor was enhanced in the 17th century by the Baroque masters: Ragi (stuccos), Pietro da Cortona (altar, right-hand transept), Andrea Pozzo (chapel of

St Ignatius of Loyola) and Baciccia (frescos).

★ Palazzo Farnese (A C4)
→ Piazza Farnese, 67
Tel. 06 68 60 11 Mon and Thu (three visits per day) by written appt only; closed end July-first week Sep; plan months ahead
Fax 06 688 097 91
The impressive façade has the austerity of a Renaissance palace. Begun by Sangallo the Younger in 1517, followed by Michelangelo in 1546, the palace was completed in 1589 by Giacomo della Porta. Frescos by Annibale and Augustino Carracci decorate the sumptuous interior. Today it houses the French Embassy.

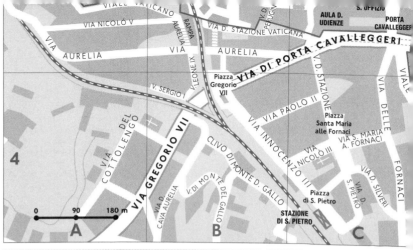

MUSEI VATICANI/CAPPELLA SISTINA

MUSEI VATICANI/CORTILE DELLA PIGNA

★ Piazza
San Pietro (B C3)

A brilliant design by Bernini. In 1656 Alexander VII asked him to design a piazza that would allow the enormous crowds to see the pope grant his *Urbi et Orbi* blessing (to the city and to the world) from the central loggia. The result was this stunning ellipse-shaped piazza, lined with two impressive colonnades, crowned with 140 statues of the saints and forming a portico wide enough to let carriages pass. Wonderful view of St Peter's from Via della Conciliazione. Papal blessing on Sundays at noon, except in summer.

★ Basilica
di San Pietro (B C3)

→ *Piazza San Pietro*
Tel. 06 69 88 34 62
Open daily:
Basilica and tombs 7am–6pm (7pm in summer);
Treasury Museum 8am–5pm (6pm in summer);
Dome 8am–sunset
The 'greatest church in Christendom' is an extraordinary feat of architectural design. The scale of this building is astounding: the 615-ft-long nave seems to unfold in front of you as you walk through. The cupola, supported by four colossal pillars, is a dizzying 450 ft high. In the 16th century, Julius II decided to rebuild

Constantine's 4th-century basilica, which stood on the burial place of St Peter. A succession of excellent architects contributed to the design. Bramante is responsible for the layout, Michelangelo for the dome and Maderno for the nave and the façade. Bernini is credited for much of the interior work, including the bronze reliquary throne *(catedra petri)*, containing what is believed to be St Peter's original wooden chair, the huge bronze *baldacchino* (canopy) and the tombs of popes Urban VIII and Alexander VII. Don't miss: the medieval statue of St Peter, whose feet have

been worn away by the kisses of generations of pilgrims; the extremely moving *Pietà* (1498–15 by the young Michelang and the grotto housing papal tombs. Climb up the drum balcony for a sense of the true size of dome and continue up 330 steps for an unbea view of the city and the Vatican gardens.

★ Giardini Vaticani
→ *Tel. 06 69 88 46 76*
Two-hour guided tours b (contact the tourist office Tue, Thu and Sat 10am–. (Sat only in Nov-Feb)
The Vatican gardens co of Italian-style gardens (dotted with grottos, st

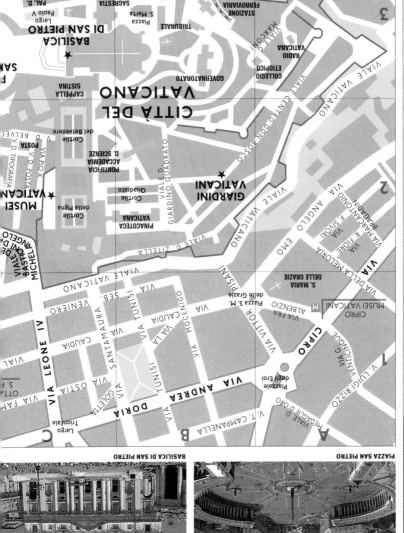

BASILICA DI SAN PIETRO

PIAZZA SAN PIETRO

The impressive beauty and perfect proportions of Piazza San Pietro certainly warrant a pause in the shadows of Bernini's colonnade. You will need to make your way through groups of pilgrims to gain entry to St Peter's Basilica and the Vatican museums. Outside the walls of the Vatican is the Prati district, and the busy, shop-lined Via Cola di Rienzo. Further north the district becomes increasingly residential: pretty streets lined with hollyhocks and rose of sharon. South of Via Cola, the imposing Castel Sant' Angelo stands by the river. Built originally as a mausoleum by Hadrian, it became a fortress, then served as a barracks and a prison, until it was turned into a papal residence and museum.

TRE PUPAZZI

DAL TOSCANO

RESTAURANTS, PIZZERIAS

Non Solo Pizza (**B** D1)
→ *Via degli Scipioni, 95-97*
Tel. 06 372 58 20
Tue-Sun 8.30am–9.30pm
Delicious slices of pizza sold *al taglio* (by weight): mushrooms, broccoli, porcini, sausages... Around €10/kg.

Osteria dell'Angelo (*off* **B** B1)
→ *Via G. Bettolo, 24-32 (on from Via T. Campanella)*
Tel. 06 372 94 70
Mon-Sat 8–11pm (also Tue-Fri 1–2.30pm)
The manager is a former rugby player and rugby shirts cover the walls of this osteria. It's a little out of the way, but the food is certainly worth the trip: wild-boar sausages, *tonarello* (pasta with peppered goat's cheese). À la carte at lunch; set menu in the evenings €25 (incl. wine). Also has a terrace. No credit cards. Reservations advised.

Tre Pupazzi (**B** E2)
→ *Borgo Pio, 183*
Tel. 06 686 83 71
Mon-Sat noon–3pm, 7–11pm
A 17th-century taverna behind Castel Sant'Angelo. The signature dish is the wonderful *cuscinetto ai Tre Pupazzi* (cheese and

prosciutto between slices of veal, with lemon sauce). À la carte €20–25.

Dal Toscano (**B** D1)
→ *Via Germanico, 58-60*
Tel. 06 397 233 73
Tue-Sun 12.30–3pm, 8–10pm
A palatable trip to Tuscany. Soup, fresh homemade pasta (try the pumpkin ravioli) and meat specialties such as *tagliata di manzo all' aceto balsamico* (beef with balsamic vinegar). À la carte €30–35.

Benito e Gilberto al Falco (**B** D2)
→ *Via del Falco, 19*
Tel. 06 686 77 69
Tue-Sat 7.30–11.30pm
A tiny, family-run seafood restaurant, opened in 1975. If you believe the photos on the walls, Mastroiani, Fellini and other celebrities have been regulars here. Seafood dishes, *fagiolini ai frutti di mare* (seafood and bean soup) and grilled fish. Reservations advised. À la carte €40–50.

Il Simposio (**B** F2)
→ *Piazza Cavour, 16*
Tel. 06 321 15 02
Mon-Fri 1–4pm, 8pm–1am; Sat 8pm–1am
The restaurant is attached to the Enoteca Costantini so there are over 300 wines on the menu, many available *al bicquiere* (by

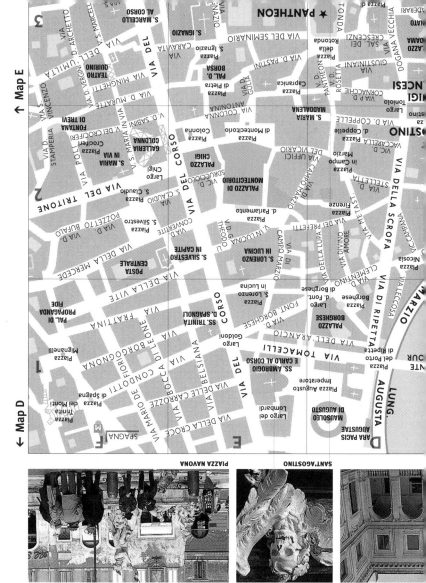

PIAZZA NAVONA

SANT'AGOSTINO

...RA BAR DEL FICO SPAZIO SETTE MERCATO DI CAMPO DEI FIORI

takes food seriously. It is a meal in itself but if you still feel peckish after gorging on *carciofi*, *fagioli*, *zucchini*, *melanzane*, *funghi* and prosciutto, as a *secondi* the *rombo al forno* (baked turbot) comes highly recommended.
À la carte €40.

ICE CREAM PARLORS, CAFÉS

Cinque Lune (A C3)
→ *Corso del Rinascimento, 89. Tel. 06 688 010 05 Tue-Sun 8am–9.30pm*
Tiny *pasticceria* that, since 1902, has served the best pastries in the city: *bombe alla crema* (cream donuts), *cornetti*, *sfogliatelle* (puff pastry with ricotta and crystallized fruit filling).

Giolitti (A E2)
→ *Via Uffici del Vicario, 40 Tel. 06 699 12 43 Daily 7am–1am*
The most famous ice cream maker in Rome since 1900. Truly scrumptious scoops in 100 different flavors.

Sant' Eustachio (A D3)
→ *Piazza di Sant'Eustachio, 82. Tel. 06 68 80 20 48 Daily 8.30am–1am (1.30am Fri; 2am Sat)*
A delicate smell of coffee

wafts from this open-fronted café out into the square. Try the *grancaffè speciale*: a strong, rich black coffee. Next door, Bar Piccolo (Via del Teatro Valle) serves an amazing *caffè alla nocciola* (coffee flavored with hazelnut).

BARS, MUSIC

La Trinchetta (A B3)
→ *Via dei Banchi Nuovi, 4 Tel. 06 68 30 01 33 Daily 12.30–3pm, 8pm–2am*
Wine expert Enrico is fanatical about grappa, the spirit distilled from grapes. He stocks over 100 varieties and can list all the different flavors. Also cold meats, cheeses (Gorgonzola with figs) and a choice of wines. Sushi on Thursday evenings.

Jazz Café (A C2)
→ *Via Zanardelli, 12 Tel. 06 682 155 08 Mon-Sat 8am–2am; Sun 6pm–2am*
An exclusive, fashionable bar. Cocktails; live music in the piano bar upstairs.

Il Locale (A C3)
→ *Vicolo del Fico, 3 Tel. 06 687 74 52 Tue-Sun 10.30pm–2.30am*
Former garage, divided into several big rooms, in which newcomers to the Italian pop and rock scene come and play.

Vineria Reggio (A C4)
→ *Campo dei Fiori, 15 Tel. 06 88 80 32 68 Mon-Sat 8.30am–2am*
An appealing *vineria* (wine bar) that opens onto Campo dei Fiori. There aren't any tables inside – you sit at the bar – but if it's too busy around the counter, take your drink outside on the terrace or on the piazza.

Bar del Fico (A B3)
→ *Piazza del Fico, 26-28 Tel. 06 686 52 05 Mon-Sat 10am–2am; Sun 3pm–2am*
A bar close to Piazza Navona, in a small square at the bend of a little alley, and with a large terrace under a shady fig tree. There's a pleasant, laid-back feel to this bar.

SHOPPING

Dakota al Pantheon (A E3)
→ *Via del Seminario, 111 Tel. 06 678 76 61 Daily 9.30am–8pm (10am Sun)*
Formerly a palace, now the place for second-hand clothing, shoes, furniture and bric-à-brac.

Antichità Tanca (A D3)
→ *Salita de' Crescenzi, 12 Tel. 06 68 80 33 28 Mon-Fri 10am–1pm, 4–8pm; Sat 10am–1pm; closed Sat*

pm in summer and Mon am in winter
For over 50 years the Tanca family have collected prints of Rome by the thousand. They also sell hand-painted Neapolitan lamps, antique jewelry and more.

Spazio Sette (A D4)
→ *Via dei Barbieri, 7 Tel. 06 686 97 47 Mon 3.30–7.30pm; Tue-Sun 9.30am–1pm, 3.30–7.30pm*
In a dark alleyway leading onto the Largo Argentina, one of the most amazing designer shops in Rome. On three floors of a 16th-century palazzo, furniture and elegant household objects by the greatest designers in Italy. Stunning frescos by Giminiano (father and son) decorate the third-floor ceiling.

Ibiz (A D4)
→ *Via dei Chiavari, 39 Tel. 06 68 30 72 97 Mon-Sat 10am–7.30pm*
From the rose-shaped key ring to the huge traveling bag, the leather goods sold here are made in the workshop next door (you can see the craftsmen at work in the morning).

Mercato di Campo dei Fiori (A C4)
→ *Mon-Sat 7am–1.30pm*
A colorful flower, fruit and vegetable market on one of the city's prettiest squares.

LEA

CAFFÈ CASTRONI

SPAZIO CORTO MALTESE

the glass). The decor is early 20th-century and the cuisine very elegant, with fantastic cheeses and charcuterie. À la carte €45–50.

ICE CREAM PARLOR, CREAMERY

Gelateria Old Bridge (**B** C2)
➜ *Viale dei Bastioni di Michelangelo, 5*
Tel. 06 397 230 26 Mon-Sat 10am-2am; Sun 3pm-2am
Every weekend locals line up in front of this tiny ice cream shop. Specialties: *cassata siciliana* (ground almond, crystallized fruit, ricotta), *zuppa inglese* (custard), *crema della nonna* (pine nut and cream). Generous serving.

Latteria di Borgo Pio (**B** D2)
➜ *Via Borgo Pio, 48*
Tel. 06 68 80 39 55 Mon-Sat 7am-9pm
With a huge wooden fridge, a marble counter and old tiled floor, this creamery in the quaint pedestrianized Via Borgo Pio feels like it's from another age. The espresso drinkers rub shoulders with the local loafers as they watch the nuns, tourists and Romans pass by.

CINEMA, BARS, MUSIC VENUES

Cinema Azzuro Scipioni (**B** D1)
➜ *Via degli Scipioni, 82*
Tel. 06 39 73 71 61
Retrospectives of work by the great filmmakers, in a small independent movie theater. The Chaplin Room (recent films, 140 seats) is decorated with odds and ends, including airplane seats. The Lumière Room seats 60 and shows old classics on a screen no bigger than a bedspread.

Alexanderplatz (**B** C1)
➜ *Via Ostia, 9*
Tel. 06 39 74 21 71 Sep-May, daily 9pm-2am www.alexanderplatz.it
Concerts by the biggest names on the Italian and international jazz scene. Reservations necessary.

Fonclea (**B** E2)
➜ *Via Crescenzio 82a*
Tel. 06 689 63 02 Sep-May, Mon-Sat 7pm-2am (3am Sat)
Pub-restaurant-live music venue – a combination that has endured here since the late seventies. Concerts every night: pop, rock or jazz.

The Place (**B** E2)
➜ *Via Alberico II, 27-29*
Tel. 06 68 21 52 14

Tue-Sun 7.30pm (bar), 8pm-2am (show and restaurant)
A chic place where you can snack on tapas, pizza and *focacce* or sit down to a gastronomic menu (€40) whilst listening to jazz, soul or rhythm 'n' blues. Entrance fee varies according to the program.

SHOPPING

Mercato della Piazza dell'Unità (**B** D1)
➜ *Via Cola di Rienzo Mon-Sat 7am-1pm*
An array of meat, dairy products and colorful fruit and vegetable stalls in an amazing covered marketplace. In summer: San Marzano (green plum tomatoes); zucchini flowers; borlotti beans.

Doctor Music (**B** D1)
➜ *Via dei Gracchi, 41-43*
Tel. 06 320 05 43 Mon-Sat 9.30am-1pm, 4-7.30pm
This music store is best known for its extensive jazz section, but it also carries rock, new age, folk and blues. Vinyl department. New and second-hand CDs.

Enoteca Costantini (**B** F2)
➜ *Piazza Cavour, 16*
Tel. 06 320 35 75

Mon 4.30-8pm; Tue-Sat 9am-1pm, 4.30-8pm
The best Italian wines, categorized by region. Downstairs is a cellar with endless vaults and thousands of bottles.

Spazio Corto Maltese (**B** E1)
➜ *Via Margutta, 96*
Tel. 06 32 65 05 15 Mon-Sat 9.30am-1pm, 4-7.30pm
A tiny bookstore specializing in comic-strip books and mainly first-edition copies of the works of Hugo Pratt (who created the character Corto Maltese).

Caffè Castroni (**B** D1)
➜ *Via Ottaviano, 55*
Tel. 06 39 72 32 79 Mon-Sat 7.30am-8pm
Excellent grocery store. Preserves, cakes, pastries, coffees and over 100 types of candy. At the counter: cappuccino (so creamy!), *panini* and *tramezzini*.

Vestiastock (**B** D1)
➜ *Via Germanico, 170a*
Tel. 06 322 43 91 Mon 3.30-7.30pm; Tue-Sat 10am-2.30pm, 3.30-7.30pm
Designer clothing for men and women at a 30-50% discount: Armani, Cerutti, Versace, Valentino etc.

LUNG. TOR DI NONA
PONTE S. ANGELO
OSPEDALE S. SPIRITO
LUNG. D...
...SSIA
BORGO S. SPIRITO
PONTE S. ANGELO FIUME TEVERE
LUNG. VATICANO
VIA DELLA CONCILIAZIONE
PALL. DEI PENITENZIERI
VIA PFEIFFER
VIA RUSTICUCCI
Piazza Pio XII
LUNG. CASTELLO
VIA TRIBONIANO
MAUSOLEO DI ADRIANO
Piazza Pia
S. MARIA IN TRASPONTINA
PALAZZO TORLONIA
BORGO SANT'ANGELO
VIA D. CORRIDORI
...ato
CASTEL SANT'ANGELO
PIAZZA ADRIANA
VIA ADRIANA
...eonina
...za
V. LEONINA
BORGO PIO
VIA PIO
Largo P. Castello
BORGO SANT'ANGELO
V.LO D. PALLINE
VIA DE OMBRELLARI
VIA TRE PUPAZZI
VIA DEL MASCHERINO
V. DI BORGO PIO
VIA PLAUTO
V. D. FALCO
PIAZZA ADRIANA
VIA P. DELLA VALLE
VIA ALBERICO II
VIA SFORZA PALLAVICINI
VIA CANCELLIERI
VIA V.G. VITELLESCHI
Cappelari
Piazza V. S. PORCARI
V.G. PORCARI
VIA CRESCENZIO
VIA CRESCENZIO
VIA BOEZIO
VIA ORAZIO
VIA VIRGILIO
VIA TERENZIO
VIA TIBULLO
VIA PROPERZIO
MUSEO STORICO DELL'ARMA D. CARABINIERI
del ...ento
PRATI
VIA CICERONE
VE. O. VISCONTI
VIA TACITO
VIA PLINIO
VIA COLA DI RIENZO
VIA COLA DI RIENZO
VIA DEI GRACCHI
Piazza d. Unità
VIA SILLA
VIA DEI GRACCHI
VIA CATONE
VIA COLA DI RIENZO
RIENZO
Piazza Cola di Rienzo
VIA A. FARNESE
VIA POMPEO MAGNO
VIA A. COLONNA
SCIPIONI
VIA EZIO
VIA PAOLO EMILIO
VIA MARIO
SAN GIOACCHINO
Piazza del Quiriti
VIA DEI GRACCHI
VIA GERMANICO
VIA CAIO MARIO
GERMANICO
SS. ROSARIO
VIA DEGLI SCIPIONI
VIA GIULIO
VIA EZIO
VIA DEGLI
VIA FABIO MASSIMO
VIA GERMANICO
CESARE
V. BARLETTA
VIA GIULIO
F
E
D
2
1

GIARDINI VATICANI

MUSEI VATICANI

MUSEI VATICANI/PINACOTECA

INSASSIA
EMANUELE II ALTOVI...
CENTRO STORICO

Piazza P. Paoli
PONTE PR.
Piazza Della Rovere
AMEDEO SAVOIA ACCIAIOLI
AOSTA
VIA D. CORONARI
Largo Tassoni
PAL. TAVERNA
VIA D. FIORENTINI
Piazza d. Orologio
COLLEGIO URBANO DI PROPAGANDA FIDE
PALAZZO SACCHETTI
PAL. SFORZA CESARINI
CHIESA NUOVA
Piazza della Chiesa Nuova
PAL. SALVIATI
Piazza di S. Onofrio
S. MARIA DEL SUFFRAGIO
VIA D. PELLEGRINO
OSPEDALE DEL BAMBIN GESÙ
FIUME TEVERE
GIANICOLENSE
VIA D. ORTI D'ALIBERT
PONTE G. MAZZINI
Largo L. Perosi

Map C →

L SANT'ANGELO

PONTE SANT'ANGELO

...ains and monuments), ...h-style gardens (with ...y planted flowerbeds), ...ds and even a kitchen ...en. All offer a stunning ...of the basilica's apse ...ransept.

usei Vaticani (B C2)
ale Vaticano
6 69 88 46 76
h-Oct: Mon-Fri 8.45am–m; Sat 8.45am–1.20pm. eb: Mon-Sat 8.45am–pm. Exit 60 mins after ng times. Free last Sun of h 8.45am–12.20pm. /mv.vatican.va
Vatican museums e an enormous ction that warrants al visits. To regulate ow of visitors, viewing is by a pre-designated arrow-marked route which ends at the Sistine Chapel (Cappella Sistina). Must see: the 395-ft-long Galleria delle Carte Geografiche (Map Gallery), hung with a series of brightly colored regional maps of Italy (16th century); the Gallerie delle Sculture with the world's most important collection of classical sculptures; the Stanze di Raffaello (Raphael Rooms), the apartments of Julius II, redecorated by Raphael in 1508, which depict the principal themes of knowledge; and the famous Pinacoteca with its rich collection of paintings from the Middle Ages right up to present day (Pinturicchio's *Virgin and Child*, Caravaggio's *Descent from the Cross* and *Christ's Burial*, Da Vinci's *St Jerome*, and Raphael's last work, *The Transfiguration*). The Sistine Chapel closes the tour. The glorious ceiling, no doubt Michelangelo's masterpiece, took four years to complete (1508–12) and has, over recent years, been meticulously restored to its former glory.

★ **Castel Sant'Angelo** (B F2)
→ Lungotevere Castello, 50
Tel. 06 681 91 11
Tue-Sun 9am–7.30pm
Hadrian's mausoleum (AD 123) became a fortress and a prison in the Middle Ages, and a papal residence in the 16th century. It is linked to St Peter's by a long passageway. The most sumptuous apartments are those of Clemente VII and Paul III, built during the years 1520–30. From the terrace, which is overshadowed by a huge bronze statue of St Michael (1752), there are fabulous views of St Peter's, il Campo di Marzo, il Gianicolo and the lovely Ponte Sant'Angelo, decorated with ten angels made of white marble. Each carries an instrument of the martyrdom of Christ.

ISOLA TIBERINA

PIAZZA MATTEI

[Map area with street names and labels:]
SPROVIERI
ROSSETTI
Piazza
VIA R. R. Pilo
G. Berchet
GIOVAGNOLI
VIA M. QUADRIO
S. MARIA
REG. PACIS
VIA F. TORRE
Piazza
Ippolito
Nievo
VIA
COLAUTTI
VIA G.
VIA ANTONIO CESARI
VIA GIULIO BARRILI
VIA A. MARIO
VIA D.
GUERRAZZI
V. FRATELLI
VIA F. DALL'ONGARO
Largo
F. Anzani
Piazza V. C. PISACANE
Oriani
VIA I. NIEVO
Largo
Alessandro
Toja
V. F. ROSAZZA
VIA GUIDO GUINIZELLI
VIA GIULIO BARRILI
VIA ALESSANDRO
V. A. TRAVERSARI
V. C. PASCARELLA
VIA N. BETTONI
VIA PONZIANO
VIALE DI TRASTEVERE
V. C. PORTA
VIA ETTORE ROLLI
VIA B. PASSERI
TEST
VIA LORENZO VALLA
V. G. PARRASIO
V. STADIVARI
V. PANFILO CASTALDI
VIA VINCENZO
MONTI
SS. PATR.
D'ITALIA
V. D'ORTI
DI CESARE
SACRO
CUORE
0   110   220 m
CIRCONV.
GIANICOLENSE
Piazza
F. Biondo
V. A. BELLANI
STAZIONE TRASTEVERE
A   B

★ Passeggiata del Gianicolo (C A2)
A walk on Janiculum hill offers you a series of breathtaking views of the city. At the center of Piazzale G. Garibaldi an equestrian statue presides in honor of the hero of the unification of Italy. Next, you arrive at the stunning Renaissance Villa Lante. Further along the ridge is the lighthouse, designed by Manfredo Manfredi, a gift from Argentina to Italy in 1911. At night it throws a beam of light in the colors of the Italian flag onto the city. The walk ends at Sant'Onofrio.

★ Isola Tiberina (C C3)
Legend has it that the island's shape is that of a boat that departed from Greece in search of Aesculapius (the god of medicine) and returned with a serpent, symbol of the god, which escaped into the Tiber. The boat remained, petrified, in the middle of the river. Since the 16th century, the island has been almost entirely occupied by the Fatebene-fratelli hospital (with a lovely Baroque church). The walk along the banks – past the Ponte Rotto (the 'broken bridge') that fell in the 16th century – is very pleasant.

★ Santa Maria in Trastevere (C B3)
→ *Piazza Santa Maria in Trastevere. Tel. 06 581 48 02 Daily 7.30am–9pm*
On an attractive little square in Trastevere's old village, the Santa Maria basilica (12th century) has preserved its medieval character. The façade is adorned with a Byzantine-influenced mosaic (12th–14th century), while the interior layout has three naves and a choir, richly decorated with mosaics: six panels are by Cavallini (13th century), the bright coloring taken from a fresco-painting technique.

★ Piazza Mattei (C ▮)
In the 16th century the Mattei family erected several palaces on this square, including Pala▮ Mattei di Giove (1598) the courtyard (Via Cae▮ 32) is a splendid colle▮ of ancient marble stat▮ At the piazza's center the elegant Fontana d▮ Tartarughe (the 'tortois▮ fountain'), designed b▮ Giacomo Della Porta (▮

★ Villa Farnesina (C ▮
→ *Via della Lungara, 23▮ Tel. 06 68 02 72 68 Mon-Sat 9am–1pm*
One of Rome's most gl▮ Renaissance, built by Peruzzi for papal finan▮

C

From Piazza Mattei, where a half-open window will allow you to catch a glimpse of a fresco or coffered ceiling, walk down toward Teatro di Marcello. You are in the heart of the Ghetto, the Jewish district. A small passageway takes you to Via d'Ottavia, lined with Jewish bakeries and restaurants. Cross the Ponte Garibaldi to reach the west bank of the Tiber and enter the busy Trastevere district, a maze of small streets, tiny squares, bars and restaurants which have become the stomping ground for young artists. Further south, and back on the east side of the river, stands Monte Testaccio, an ancient landfill surrounded by lively bars and clubs.

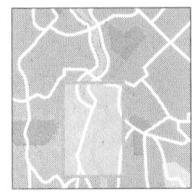

DA GIGETTO   CHECCHINO DAL 1887

RESTAURANTS, PIZZERIAS

'Da Oio' a Casa Mia (C C5)
→ Via Galvani, 43-45
Tel. 06 578 26 80 Mon-Sat
noon–3.30pm, 7– 12.30am
A Testaccio restaurant that maintains a family-like welcome. Pasta (gnocchi, rigatoni alla pajata, tonarelli al cacio e pepe) and for secondi: tripe and braised oxtail. À la carte €20–30.

Al Pompiere (C D2)
→ Palazzo Cenci Bolognetti, via di Santa Maria de' Calderari, 38
Tel. 06 686 83 77 Mon-Sat
12.30–3pm, 7.30–11pm
A staircase leads to a huge room with fresco-painted ceilings. In the heart of the Ghetto, within the 16th-century Beatrice Cenci palace, Al Pompiere specializes in Jewish food and fried dishes (brains, offal, fish). For dessert: crostata di ricotta e visciole (cheesecake with sour cherries). À la carte €25–35.

Da Lucia (C B3)
→ Vicolo del Mattonato, 2b
Tel. 06 580 36 01 Tue-Sun
12.30–3pm, 7.30–11pm
The grandmother who ran this trattoria since 1938 is now no longer around, but the place has retained its laid-back hospitality. Spaghetti al cacio e pepe (ewe's cheese with peppercorns), gnocchi, Roman tripe and cod. À la carte €30–35.

Da Gigetto Al Portico d'Ottavia (C D2)
→ Via del Portico d'Ottavia, 21a. Tel. 06 686 11 05
Tue-Sun 12.15–3pm, 7.30–11pm
This large inn with a terrace and rustic dining rooms is an institution. Try the excellent carciofi alla giudia (fried Jewish-style artickoke hearts) or any of the other Roman-Jewish specialties. Reservations necessary. À la carte €35.

Enoteca Ferrara (C B2)
→ Via del Moro, 1a
Tel. 06 583 339 20
Daily 6pm–2am (wine bar); 8–11.30pm (restaurant); 10am–2am (shop)
Bright, lively wine bar in a 17th-century palazzo, with painted faience dining tables and offering a delicate cuisine. Smart catalogs will help you choose one of the 1,000 Italian wines on offer. À la carte €40–45.

Checchino dal 1887 (C C6)
→ Via Monte Testaccio, 30
Tel. 06 574 63 18
Tue-Sun 12.30–3pm, 8pm–

Map B →

PASSEGGIATA DEL GIANICOLO

VILLA FARNESINA

SANTA MARIA IN TRASTEVERE

ECA FERRARA **VOLPETTI** **MERCATO DI PORTA PORTESE**

midnight. Closed in August and for a week at Christmas
A smart, superior bistro serving top-quality Roman cuisine. Wide choice of cheeses and an incredible wine list that represents the best wines from all over Italy. Reservations advisable. À la carte €50.

Alberto Ciarla (C B3)
→ *Piazza San Cosimato, 40 Tel. 06 581 86 68 Mon-Sat 8.30pm–midnight*
A highly-praised restaurant with a lavish decor and an original cuisine – the recipes have been handed from father to son for the past century. Smoked or raw fish, *minestra portolana* (soup with pasta, seafood and vegetables), pasta, grilled meats. Extensive list of regional desserts and a long wine list. Carte and gastronomic set menus: €50–90. Reservations advisable.

ICE CREAM PARLOR, PATISSERIES

Forno del Ghetto (C D2)
→ *Via del Portico d'Ottavia, 1 Tel. 06 687 86 37 Sun-Thu 7.30am–7.30pm; Fri 7.30am–4pm*
This tiny patisserie is one of the best known in the city: Kosher pizza,

cookies (*biscottini, ginetti, amaretti*) and the famous *torta di ricotta e visciole* (sour-cherry cheesecake).

Sacchetti (C B3)
→ *Piazza San Cosimato, 61-62 Tel. 06 581 53 74 Tue-Sun 5.30am–11.30pm*
A bar, pastry shop and ice cream parlor in one. Try their *torta ungherese*. Summer terrace with beautiful views over the Trastevere.

CINEMA, BARS, MUSIC VENUES

Cinema Arena Nuovo Sacher (C C4)
→ *Largo Aschianghi, 1 Tel. 06 581 81 16 Daily*
Nani Moretti's movie theater shows Italian and foreign films which are not usually on wide release. Films in their original language on Mon. Open-air movie festival in summer.

Bibli (C C3)
→ *Via dei Fienaroli, 28 Tel. 06 588 40 97 Mon 5.30pm–midnight; Tue-Sun 11am–midnight*
A quiet haven tucked away in a back street in Trastevere: bookstore (with Internet access), readings, conferences. It's possible to eat on the patio. Brunch at the

weekend, €16.

Oasi della Birra (C B6)
→ *Piazza Testaccio, 38-40 Tel. 06 574 61 22 Daily 7.30pm–2am (bar); 8am–1.30pm, 4–7.30pm (shop)*
A wine store with over 500 wines and 600 beers from all over the world: *Superbaladin* (double malt) and *Menabrea* (white beer). In the basement is a remarkable restaurant built on ancient Roman remains and serving Northern Italian specialties. Plus 40 varieties of ham and 85 different cheeses.

Big Mama (C C4)
→ *Vicolo San Francesco a Ripa, 18 Tel. 06 581 25 51 Tue-Sat 9pm–1.30am*
Rome's temple to the blues since 1984.

Monte Testaccio (C C6)
Akab (no. 69)
→ *Tel. 06 57 25 05 85 Wed-Sat 10pm–4am*
Live music: soul, dance, R 'n' B and house.
L'Alibi (no. 44)
→ *Tel. 06 574 34 48 Wed-Sun 11.30pm–5am*
Gay club; more of a mixed crowd in summer. Terrace.

Bartaruga (C D2)
→ *Piazza Mattei, 9 Tel. 06 689 22 99 Mon-Sat 5pm–2am*
A bar with an astonishing

decor of royal blue walls and gilded moldings. When the bar is full, or when it's warm, sit outside on the piazza by the Fontana delle Tartarughe. Low-key music and a discerning crowd.

SHOPPING

Volpetti (C D5)
→ *Via Marmorata, 47 Tel. 06 574 23 52 Mon-Sat 8am–2pm, 5–8.15pm*
Testaccio's most famous deli, and one of the best in town. The counters groan under the weight of the dozens of cheeses, hams, pasta and olive oils.

Mercato Testaccio (C C5)
→ *Mon-Sat 8am–1pm*
With stalls selling brand-name shoes at very good prices (Wed and Sat), this is one of the city's most successful markets. Less picturesque, perhaps, than the market on Campo dei Fiori, but more authentically Roman.

Mercato di Porta Portese (C C4)
→ *Porta Portese / Via Portuense Sun 7am–2pm*
Clothes, furniture, music, scooter parts and gadgets of all sorts at low prices. Busy market and a real slice of Roman life.

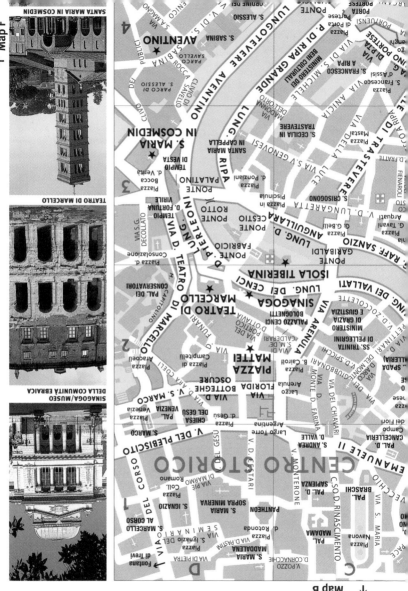

Villa Borghese is a magical place where, under the shade of the huge trees, the Romans once sought refuge from the summer heat. Next is Pincio hill, overlooking the city and, in the background, the dome of St Peter. Beneath you is the Piazza del Popolo, the starting point for the three artery roads which branch out to form the Tridente; here you can find luxury boutiques, chic cafés and the best names in fashion. At the far end is the Via del Babuino, Piazza di Spagna and the marvelous steps leading to Trinità dei Monti, a setting that is close to perfection. The Spanish Steps provide a favorite meeting place for tourists and locals alike.

OTELLO ALLA CONCORDIA

IL MARGUTTA

RESTAURANTS, PIZZERIAS

Fior Fiore (**D** C4)
→ Via della Croce, 17-18
Tel. 06 679 13 86
Daily 11am–8pm (11.30pm Tue-Sun in summer)
Close to Piazza di Spagna, excellent pizza al taglio. Thirty types on offer, including the terrific pizza al radicchio (red endive) or pizza with zucchini flowers. Plus breadsticks, pasta, ice cream etc.

Otello alla Concordia (**D** C4)
→ Via della Croce, 81
Tel. 06 679 11 78 Mon-Sat 12.30–3pm, 7.30–11pm
Classic Roman cuisine al fresco, in a marvelous little green courtyard. Set menu €20.

Il Margutta (**D** C3)
→ Via Margutta, 118
Tel. 06 326 505 77 Daily noon–3.30pm, 7–11.30pm
One of the first and one of very few vegetarian restaurants in Rome. Varied, flavorsome cuisine using seasonal produce and innovative dishes. The exhibitions of contemporary art on the large walls, the comfortable black leather seating lend the place a chic feel. Brunch on Sun. À la carte €30–40.

'Gusto (**D** B4)
→ Piazza Augusto Imperatore, 9
Tel. 06 322 6273 Daily 12.30–3pm, 7.30pm–midnight (wine bar and store 10am–1am)
At the foot of the Augustus mausoleum, an Italian-style shopping mall which is very food orientated. Restaurant, pizzeria, wine bar and stores (wine, cigars and a bookstore dedicated to cook books). In the restaurant: Italian dishes, Middle Eastern (couscous) and Asian food. À la carte €40. On the ground floor you will be able to snack on numerous types of pizza, bruschette etc. Brunch (Sat-Sun) from €14

Penna d'Oca (**D** B3)
→ Via della Penna, 53
Tel. 06 320 28 98
Mon-Sat 8pm–11.30pm
Creative cooking with an accent on fish dishes, and desserts from southern Italy. Intimate setting and attractive terrace, just two minutes from Piazza del Popolo. More than 400 wines from around the world. À la carte €40–45.

Antico Bottaro (**D** B3)
→ Passeggiata di Ripetta, 15
Tel. 06 323 67 63
Thu-Tue 8–10.30pm
Refined international cuisine with a French and Italian slant. Attractive

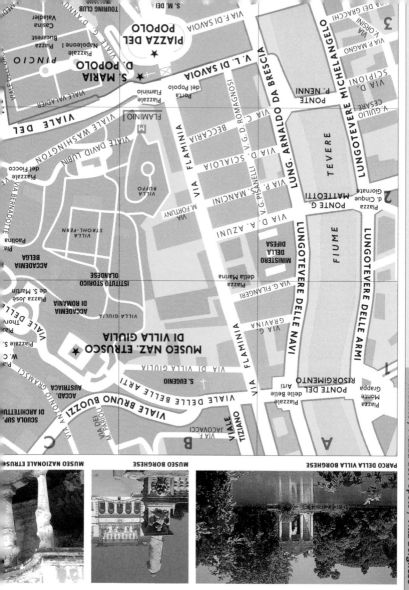

MUSEO NAZIONALE ETRUSC

MUSEO BORGHESE

PARCO DELLA VILLA BORGHESE

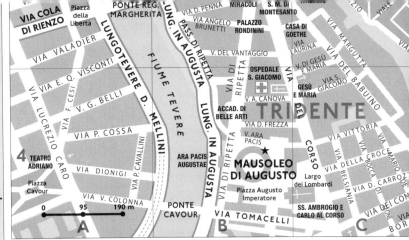

VIA COLA
DI RIENZO

Piazza
della
Libertà

PONTE REG.
MARGHERITA

VIA D. PENNA
VIA ANGELO
BRUNETTI

MIRACOLI   S. M. DI
MONTESANTO

PALAZZO
RONDININI

CASA DI
GOETHE

VIA MARGUTTA

VIALE

VIA VALADIER

VIA E. Q. VISCONTI

VIA F. CESI

VIA P. COSSA

LUNGOTEVERE D. MELLINI

FIUME TEVERE

VIA DI RIPETTA

PASS. DI RIPETTA

V. DEL VANTAGGIO

OSPEDALE
S. GIACOMO

VIA
LAURINA

V. DI GESÙ
E MARIA

VIA DI RIPETTA

V. A. CANOVA

ACCAD. DI
BELLE ARTI

GESÙ
E MARIA

VIA S.
GIACOMO

VIA DEL BABUINO

LUCREZIO CARO

VIA G. BELLI

VIA P. CAVALLINI

LUNG. IN AUGUSTA

VIA D. FREZZA

TRIDENTE

4 TEATRO
   ADRIANO

VIA DIONIGI

Piazza
Cavour

VIA V. COLONNA

ARA PACIS
AUGUSTAE

V. ARA
PACIS

MAUSOLEO
DI AUGUSTO

Largo
dei Lombardi

CORSO

VIA VITTORIA

VIA DELLA CROCE

VIA MARIO DE

VIA BELSIANA

VIA D. CARROZ

VIA DEI CON

0   95   190 m

PONTE
CAVOUR

VIA TOMACELLI

Piazza Augusto
Imperatore

SS. AMBROGIO E
CARLO AL CORSO

BOR

A   B   C

PIAZZA DEL POPOLO

MAUSOLEO DI AUGUSTO

★ Parco della Villa Borghese (D D2)

One of Rome's largest and loveliest parks, created in 1605 by Scipione Borghese. Visit the temple of Aesculapius (18th century) and the lake, as well as Piazza di Siena, with its grass-covered amphitheater. Around the Casino, the citrus grove (140 species), the bulb garden (crocus, narcissus, hyacinth) and the meridian garden (violets and tulips) are all of interest.

★ Villa Giulia (Museo Nazionale Etrusco) (D C1)

→ Piazza di Villa Giulia, 9
Tel. 06 322 65 71
Tue–Sun 8.30am–7.30pm

Pope Julius III's splendid summer villa, built in 1551 by Vignola and Ammannati, has been home to Rome's Etruscan museum since 1889. It exhibits ceramics, jewelry, bronze statues and earthenware from the necropolis of the Latium (5th and 6th century BC). The semicircular portico is a treasure: trompe l'œil arbors open onto the villa's Italian-style garden.

★ Museo e Galleria Borghese (D F2)

→ Piazza Scipione Borghese
Tel. 06 06 328 101 Tue–Sun
9am–7pm (by appt only)
The museum and gallery Borghese contain works by Raphael, Titian, Coreggio,

Caravaggio and a sculpture gallery with magnificent works by Bernini – Apollo and Daphne (1622–5), The Rape of Prosperpina (1621–2) – and Canova's Pauline Borghese (1805–8), Napoleon's sister posing as Venus. Cardinal Scipione Borghese, a ruthless art lover, had his Casino extended to hold his private collection (including works he 'looked after' for the men he had imprisoned). It is, without doubt, the most exquisite private collection in Rome.

★ Galleria Nazionale d'Arte Moderna (D D1)

→ Via delle Belle Arti, 131
Tel. 06 322 981

Tue–Sun 8.30am–7.30pm
This gallery presents on
of the most interesting
collections of 19th- and
20th-century Italian
sculpture and painting
works from the neoclas
Romantic, Futurist scho
and even the Novecent
(20th century) school:
Chirico, Morandi, Marin

★ Santa Maria del Popolo (D B3)

→ Piazza del Popolo, 12
Tel. 06 361 08 36
Daily 7am–12.15pm, 4–7.
Renaissance church
refurbished by some of
Italy's most important
architects (Bernini, Rap
Fontana). On opposite
of the Cerasi chapel ha

D

AVENTINO/SANTA SABINA

TESTACCIO

tino Chigi, who called
n the greatest artists of
ime to decorate it. On
round floor are frescos
aphael (*The Myth of
he* and *The Myth of
ea*). Above is the
 delle Prospettive
pectives) with its
pe-l'œil fresco views
th-century Rome, by
zzi himself.

nagoga (C D2)
ostra permanente della
ınità Israelitica, Lung.
enci. Tel. 06 68 40 06 61
 Thu 9am–7.30pm (5pm
r); Fri 9am–1.30pm;
oam–noon
ırcheological remains
e tormented history of

Rome's oldest community,
dating back to the taking of
Jerusalem in 63 BC. In 1555
all Jews were confined to
a walled ghetto – the wall
did not fall until 1870.
Exhibition of silverware,
religious objects and prints.

★ **Teatro
di Marcello (C** D2)
→ *Via del Portico d'Ottavia, 29
Tel. 06 87 13 15 90 Tours by
appt; concerts June-Oct at
8.30pm*
This grandiose theater,
dedicated by Augustus
(1st century BC) to his late
nephew, could hold 15,000
spectators. The portico,
dedicated to his sister,
Octavia, formed part of a

group of temples and Curia.

★ **Santa Maria in
Cosmedin (C** D3)
→ *Piazza Bocca della
Verità, 18. Daily 10am–5pm*
The touching simplicity of
this 8th-century church is
dominated by one of the
most spectacular
Romanesque campaniles in
the city. Under the portico,
visitors submit themselves
to divine judgment by
placing their hands in the
Bocca della Verità (mouth
of truth), said to bite off
the hand of any liar.

★ **Aventino (C** D4)
A hill dotted with parks and
gardens. The orange grove
in Parco Savello offers a

stunning panoramic view
of the city. Next to it is the
lovely Santa Sabina basilica
(5th century), then Piazza
dei Cavalieri di Malta
(Piazza of the Knights of
the Order of Malta), with its
church (1764–6) and villa
Take a peek through the
keyhole in the gate for a
glimpse of St Peter's dome).

★ **Testaccio (C** C6)
→ *Tel. 06 67 10 38 19
Tours by appt*
An ancient landfill (115 ft
high), formed in AD 140–250
from an accumulation of
debris. The galleries carved
into the side of the mound
contain some unusual bars,
clubs and restaurants.

CO CAFFÈ GRECO GIANNI VERSACE TAD CONCEPT STORE

Baroque decor with high leather chairs, mirrors, sculpted wooden statues and soft lighting. À la carte €60–65.

BAR, PUB, THEATER

L'EnotecAntica (D C4)
→ *Via della Croce, 76b*
Tel. 06 679 08 96 Daily: noon–midnight (restaurant); 11am–1am (wine bar)
An attractive *vineria* (wine bar) with cherub frescos on the walls and loud music. The *fragolino* (sweet red wine tasting slightly of strawberries) is worth trying. Restaurant at the back of the long wooden counter.

Gregory's Pub (D D4)
→ *Via Gregoriana, 54a*
Tel. 06 679 63 86
Tue-Sun 5.30pm–3.30am
On the ground floor is a quiet, pleasant pub. Upstairs is a low-ceilinged room with a few tables and comfortable couches, where you can hear jam sessions on Wed (international jazz musicians). It has an intimate quality, with a good rapport between audience and musicians. The bar stocks 75 different types of whiskey. On concert nights the first drink is €5–8.

Teatro Sistina (D D4)
→ *Via Sistina, 129*
Tel. 06 420 07 11 Daily 10am–7pm (tickets); Tue-Sat 9pm, Sun 5pm (shows)
A theater dedicated to musicals. Great acoustics.

CAFÉS

Antico Caffè Greco (D C4)
→ *Via Condotti, 86*
Tel. 06 679 17 00
Sun-Mon 10.30am–7pm; Tue-Sat 9am–7.30pm
Stendhal, Leopardi, Ungaretti... some of the best writers have sat in this prestigious café, founded in 1760 and tucked away between the boutiques of the Via Condotti. The interior retains its velvet chairs, marble-topped tables, red-colored walls, pictures, sculptures and tailcoated staff. Pastries, coffees and ice cream. Cheaper if you sit at the counter.

SHOPPING

Via dei Condotti (D C4)
The leading names in haute couture: **Giorgio Armani** (at no. 77), **Max Mara** (at no. 18), **Prada** (at no. 91-95).
Via Borgognona (D C4)
Parallel to Via dei Condotti: **Fendi** (at

no. 36/ 39) for leather and furs, **Laura Biagiotti** (at no. 43-44).
DA Dress Agency (D B3)
→ *Via del Vantaggio, 1b*
Tel. 06 321 08 98
Mon 4–7.30pm; Tue-Sat 10am–1pm, 4–7.30pm
Cut-price ready-to-wear and haute couture. From €5 to €2,000.
Buccone (D B4)
→ *Via di Ripetta, 19–20*
Tel. 06 361 21 54
Mon-Thu 9am–8.30pm; Fri-Sat 9am–midnight
A historic wine store with liqueurs, wines and preserves piled right up to the ceiling. It also sells gourmet food – cheeses, meats, patés etc. Pastries and prepared food can be taken out or eaten in, at one of the few tables at the rear.
C.u.c.i.n.a. (D C4)
→ *Via Mario de' Fiori, 65*
Tel. 06 679 12 75
Mon 3.30–7.30pm; Tue-Sat 10.30am–7.30pm
www.cucinastore.com
Acronym for 'How a New Cuisine Inspires New Appetites'. Stocks designer kitchen accessories: utensils for making fresh pasta and a little gem of a coffee maker (*caffetiera espresso*), which stands directly on the stove; the coffee falls directly

into the cup beside it.
Borghetto Flaminio (D B2)
→ *Piazza della Marina, 32*
Tel. 06 588 05 17
Sep-July: Sun 10am–7pm
A typical Sunday market. Books, records, bric-à-brac, and above all, clothing. Great for bargain hunters. Entrance fee €1.60.
TAD Concept Store (D C3)
→ *Via del Babuino 155a*
Tel. 06 326 951 31
Mon noon–7.30pm; Tue-Thu, Sat 10.30am–8pm; Sun noon–8pm (Oct-May)
Perfume, home furnishings, accessories, shoes – if it's hip, it's on sale here, in this two-story haven of cool design. One of the most interesting stores in Rome; The Tad Café serves breakfast and snacks.
Fabriano (D C3)
→ *Via del Babuino 173*
Tel. 06 326 00361
Mon noon–7.30pm; Tue-Sat 10am–7.30pm
Fabriano is the oldest papermill in Italy, dating back to 1264. In their store you will find stationery and accessories of a quality only achieved by the Italians – photo albums, leather notebooks, diaries, pens. Delicate, contemporary designs and exquisite packaging.

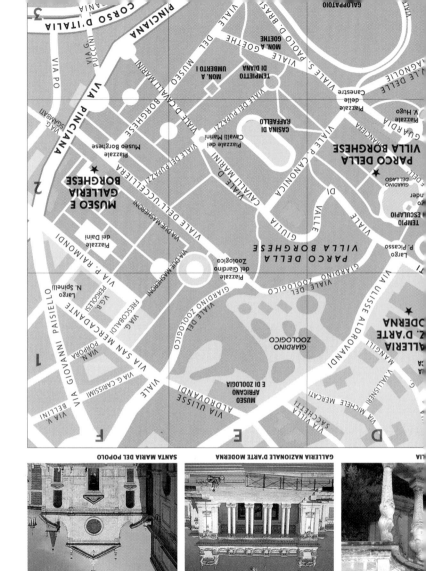

DI SPAGNA

TRINITÀ DEI MONTI

VILLA MEDICI

...asterpieces by ...aggio: *The Crucifixion* ...*Peter* (1600) and *The* ...*rsion of St Paul* (1600).

...usoleo
...gusto (D B4)
→ ...*zza Augusto Imperatore*
... 67 10 38 19 *Sat-Sun*
...–1pm (by appt only)*
...BC Augustus
...issioned a burial
... – one of the most
...essive monuments
...cient Rome. Now, all
...emains of this
...did structure are the
... of a circular building,
... in diameter,
...thed in the 1930s.

...azza del Popolo (D B3)
... early 16th century
...iazza, with Santa

Maria del Popolo on one side, was not of great interest. In 1589 Sixtus V erected an obelisk to Ramesses II, providing a centerpiece to the square. In 1675 Rainaldi added twin churches on either side of the Via del Corso. Then, in the 19th century, Valadier divided the piazza into two half-circles, erected a link to Pincio and gave coherence to the whole design. Superb views of Pincio hill.

★Piazza di Spagna (D D4)
One of the most amazing constructions in the city. The triangular-shaped piazza incorporates the Fontana della Barcaccia (1627–9, by Bernini, father

or son) and the famous terraced Spanish steps (1723, by De Sancti) leading to the church of Trinità dei Monti at the top of Pincio. At no. 26 is the Casina Rossa, where Keats (1795–1821) spent the end of his life.

★Trinità dei Monti (D D4)
→ *Piazza della Trinità dei Monti, 3. Tel. 06 679 41 79*
Daily 10am–1pm, 3–8pm
This church was founded by the French in the 16th century. It has two domed clock towers and contains a series of Mannerist frescos by Daniele da Volterra, one of which is the *Descent from the Cross*, painted after a drawing by Michelangelo. There is a breathtaking

view of Via Condotti from the front of the church.

★Villa Medici (D D3)
→ *Viale della Trinità dei Monti, 1. Tel. 06 676 11*
Exhibitions: daily 10am–8pm
Since 1804 this has been the seat of the Academy of France, a unique setting where young French artists come to complete their training. The façade leading onto the street may be austere, but the one onto the resplendent garden is luxuriously ornate. Contemporary art exhibitions are held in the garden at times, providing a good opportunity to visit this magical building, usually closed to the public.

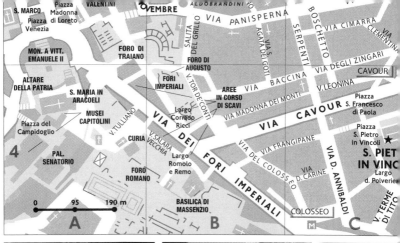

VALENTINI
Piazza
Madonna
di Loreto
Piazza
Venezia
S. MARCO
NOVEMBRE
ALDOBRANDINI
VIA PANISPERNA
BOSCHETTO
VIA CIMARRA
VIA CLEMENTINA
SALITA DEL GRILLO
VIA S. AGATA DE' GOTI
SERPENTI
MON. A VITT. EMANUELE II
FORO DI TRAIANO
FORO DI AUGUSTO
VIA DEGLI ZINGARI
CAVOUR
ALTARE DELLA PATRIA
FORI IMPERIALI
AREE IN CORSO DI SCAVI
VIA BACCINA
V.LEONINA
Piazza S. Francesco di Paola
S. MARIA IN ARACOELI
V. TOR DE'CONTI
VIA MADONNA DEI MONTI
VIA CAVOUR
MUSEI CAPITOLINI
Largo Corrado Ricci
Piazza S. Pietro in Vincoli ★
Piazza del Campidoglio
V.TULLIANO
VIA DEI FORI IMPERIALI
S. PIET IN VINC
CURIA
V.SALARA VECCHIA
Largo Romolo e Remo
VIA FRANGIPANE
Largo d. Polverier
PAL. SENATORIO
FORO ROMANO
VIA DEL COLOSSEO
VIA D. CARINE
VIA D. ANNIBALDI
0   95   190 m
BASILICA DI MASSENZIO
VIA TERME DI TITO
COLOSSEO
A   B   C

GALLERIA NAZIONALE D'ARTE ANTICA

TERME DI DIOCLEZIANO

PALAZZO MASSIMO ALLE T

★ **Fontana di Trevi** (**E** A2)
→ *Piazza di Trevi*
The famous, larger-than-life Trevi fountain by Nicolò Salvi (1762), immortalized by Fellini in his film *La Dolce Vita*. Legend has it that if you throw a coin over your shoulder into the fountain you are guaranteed to return to the Eternal City.

★ **Galleria Colonna** (**E** A3)
→ *Via della Pilotta, 17*
Tel. 06 678 43 50
Sat 9am–1pm (it is advisable to call ahead and book)
The Colonna (an old Roman family) collected a number of 15th–17th-century paintings, now on display in their palace, which also has

of the most interesting Baroque interiors in Rome.

★ **Palazzo del Quirinale** (**E** B2)
→ *Piazza del Quirinale*
Tel. 06 469 91
Sun 8.30am–noon
Papal summer residence 1592–1870. Home to Italian monarchy until 1944, when, under the Republic, the palace became the presidential seat. Almost all the Roman architects of the Counter-Reformation and Baroque era left their mark here. The spiral staircase is attributed to Mascarino (16th century). From the piazza are panoramic views of the city.

★ **Sant'Andrea al Quirinale** (**E** C2)
→ *Via del Quirinale, 29*
Tel. 06 474 08 07
Daily 8.30am (9am Sat-Sun)–noon, 3.30–7pm
Bernini's masterpiece. To overcome the lack of space he designed an elliptical-shaped church, covered by a huge dome. Light filters through the windows in the cupola, where the gilt and white stucco is in contrast to the dark, multicolored marble in the area below.

★ **San Carlo alle Quattro Fontane** (**E** C2)
→ *Via del Quirinale, 23*
Tel. 06 488 31 09
Mon-Fri 9am–1pm, 4–6pm;

Sat 9am–1pm
Borromini's first comm. in Rome, completed a his death in 1685. He overcame space restri with ingenuity, creatin tiny Baroque gem, diff from the other monum buildings of the time. continual play of conc and convex lines creat strong feeling of move in the design. Stunnin cupola: a mix of crosse octagons and hexagon

★ **Galleria Nazional d'Arte Antica** (**E** C1)
→ *Palazzo Barberini, Via delle Quattro Fontane*
Tel. 06 328 101 (reservati *Tue-Sun 9am–7pm*

E

GALLERIA COLONNA

FONTANA DI TREVI

The Esquiline, Rome's highest hill, stretches from the Coliseum to the Termini. At the top stands Santa Maria Maggiore, one of the city's four major basilicas. To the east is the increasingly cosmopolitan district around Piazza Vittorio Emanuele II. The Rione Monti district, which flanks the west of Esquilino, comprises a mass of ornate streets with numerous little churches. Further north and west is the Quirinal, offering magnificent views over the city. South again, the neighborhood around the Trevi fountain is one of the most picturesque in Rome.

EST! EST! EST!

AGATA & ROMEO

RESTAURANTS

Africa (E E1)
→ *Via Gaeta, 26*
Tel. 06 494 10 77
Tue-Sun 8am–midnight
Two minutes from Stazione Termini, excellent spicy Eritrean cuisine. Also open for breakfast (yogurt and *ful* – a type of bean stew). À la carte €10–20.

Est! Est! Est! (E C2)
→ *Via Genova, 32*
Tel. 06 488 11 07
Tue-Sun 7pm–midnight
This is reputed to be the oldest pizzeria in town, owned by the same family for four generations. The interior hasn't changed since 1920 and the Neapolitan pizzas are much appreciated by the Romans. Reservations necessary. Pizza €5–12.

Piccolo Arancio (E A2)
→ *Vicolo Scanderbeg, 112*
Tel. 06 678 61 39 Tue-Sun noon–3pm, 7pm–midnight
Magnificent risotto *al radicchio* (red endive), outstanding ravioli *d'arancio* (with orange), mouthwatering *faraona al arancio* (grouse with orange) and a good choice of fish dishes. In summer there is a pleasant terrace overlooking the piazza at the foot of Quirinale.

À la carte €20–25.

Trimani Wine Bar (E D1)
→ *Via Cernaia, 37b*
Tel. 06 446 96 30 Mon-Sat 11.30am–3pm, 5.30–12.30am
Close to the Diocletian Baths, this is a wine bar run by the oldest wine merchants in Rome. The owner also loves good food. Fresh salmon, cold meats, cheeses, homemade condiments (fruit mustards) and more than 300 different wines (from €2 a glass). Marvelous dessert cart (chestnuts in syrup, meringue and whipped cream). À la carte €30.

Hasekura (E C3)
→ *Via dei Serpenti, 27*
Tel. 06 483 648
Mon-Sat noon–2.30pm, 7–10.30pm
Understated decor and superb Japanese food: miso soup, tofu, tempura, sashimi, sushi. Lunch set menus €15. Evening à la carte €30.

Trattoria Monti (E E3)
→ *Via di San Vito 13A*
Tel. 06 44 66 573
Tue-Sat 12.30– 2.45pm, 7.30– 11pm; Sun 12.30–2.45pm
An excellent trattoria specializing in traditional cooking from the Marches region, at reasonable prices. Reservations necessary. À la carte €35.

LLA

CAFFÉ BOHÉMIEN

MERCATO ESQUILINO

Agata & Romeo (**E** E3)
→ *Via Carlo Alberto, 45*
Tel. 06 446 61 15 Mon-Fri
12.30–3.30pm, 7.30–11pm
Specialties from
Latium and Campania,
imaginative and
supremely accomplished.
Tiny ravioli with swordfish
and beans, tuna steaks
with foie gras... Over
1,500 wines. Set menus
(€100 or €150, including
wine) or à la carte €90
(the menu changes every
three months).

ICE CREAM PARLORS, CAFÉS

**Palazzo
del Freddo** (**E** F4)
→ *Via Principe Eugenio, 65-*
67 Tel. 06 446 47 40
Tue-Fri noon–midnight (1am
Sat); Sun 10am–1am
Opened in 1880, Giovanni
Fassi's 'ice palace' has
introduced generations
of Romans to the delights
of ice cream.
San Crispino (**E** A2)
→ *Via della Panetteria, 42*
Tel. 06 679 39 24
Wed-Mon noon–12.30am
(1.30am Fri-Sat)
Doubtless this is the best
ice cream parlor in Rome.
Always produced with
creative flair, the flavors
follow whatever fruits are
in season. They're

innovative (meringue),
unusual (liquorice-lemon),
basic (their signature
flavor is *crema* made with
wild Sardinian honey).
They also do a mean
zabaglione.
Panella (**E** E4)
→ *Via Merulana, 54*
Tel. 06 487 26 51
Mon-Wed, Fri-Sat 8am–2pm,
5– 8pm; Thu and Sun
8am–2pm
Bread made from unusual
ancient Roman, Sicilian
and Greek recipes *(panis
quadratus, farreus* or
nauticus...). There are over
100 of them, with rocket
and olive, Ligurian green
olive, pepperoni... It also
doubles as a coffee store
and serves morning
aperitifs. Try a Maronitta
cocktail (candied
chestnut, prosecco and
rum) as a breakfast juice
and get yourself into
true holiday mode.
Caffé Bohémien (**E** C3)
→ *Via degli Zingari, 36*
Tel. 328 173 01 58 Tue-Sat
6pm–2am (3am Fri-Sat)
Order a creamy hot
chocolate, settle yourself
in an old velvet armchair
and take a late lunch in
front of the counter, inlaid
with mirrors. Tearoom,
wine bar, art bookstore,
cultural center – it's a
place for every mood

and hour of the day.
**Antico Caffè
del Brasile** (**E** C3)
→ *Via dei Serpenti, 23*
Tel. 06 488 23 19
Mon-Sat 6am–8.30pm; Sun
7am–7pm (2pm July-Aug)
For espresso lovers: *alla
viennese* (with chocolate
and whipped cream), *alla
spagnola* (with brandy
and cream), *alla jamaica*
(with rum and cream).

OPERA

Teatro dell' Opera (**E** D2)
→ *Via Firenze, 72*
Tel. 06 48 1602 55
Tue-Sat 10am–4pm;
Sun 9.30am–1.30pm
www.opera.roma.it
Popular operas on a grand
scale. Excellent concerts
and recitals.

PUB, BAR

Fiddler's Elbow (**E** D3)
→ *Via dell' Olmata, 43*
Tel. 06 487 21 10
Daily 5pm–1.30am
The oldest and perhaps
the most famous pub
in Rome. Long bar and
typically Irish decor.
Cavour 313 (**E** C4)
→ *Via Cavour, 313*
Tel. 06 678 54 96
Mon-Sat 12.30–2.45pm,
7.30pm–12.30am (also
Sun evening Oct-June)

The ideal choice for a glass
of wine (over 1,200 from all
regions of Italy), which you
can enjoy with a plate of
various carpacci (cured
meats), daily specials and
cheeses (€15–20).

SHOPPING

Fausto Santini (**E** C4)
→ *Via Cavour, 106*
Tel. 06 488 09 34 Tue-Fri
10am–1pm, 3.30–7.30pm;
Sat 10am–1.30pm, 3–7.30pm
You shouldn't leave Rome
without a pair of Italian
shoes. Here you'll find last
season's shoes by Fausto
Santini (Giacomo's son),
on sale all year round at
half the original price or
less. The new collections
are on sale at Via Frattina,
120 (**A** F1).
Maurizio Denisi (**E** B3)
→ *Via Panisperna, 51*
Tel. 06 474 07 32
Mon-Sat 10.30am–1pm,
4–7.30pm
Piled up in this little store
(without any sign outside)
are decorative objects and
furniture from 1930 to
1940, which Maurizio
acquired all over Italy.
Mercato Esquilino (**E** F4)
→ *Via Principe Amedeo*
Mon-Sat 8am–1pm
A popular and lively market
with *alimentari* (groceries),
spices and vegetable stalls.

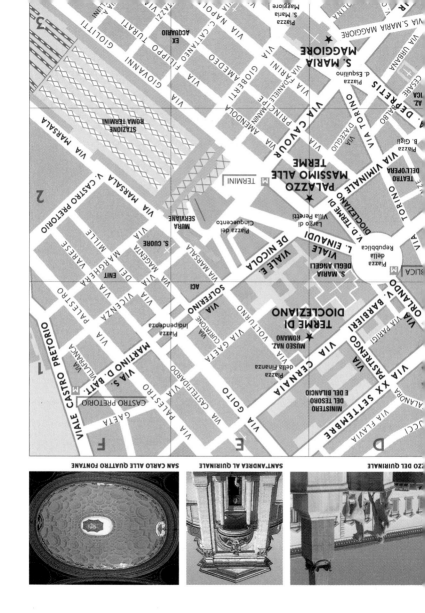

...ZZO DEL QUIRINALE   SANT'ANDREA AL QUIRINALE   SAN CARLO ALLE QUATTRO FONTANE

MARIA MAGGIORE

SAN PIETRO IN VINCOLI

ation advised)
ni, Borromini and
da Cortona were
ed in the building
splendid *palazzo*,
f the most important
ums in Rome, devoted
nting from the 13th to
entury (Perugino,
o Lippi, Caravaggio...).
3th-century works are
priately on display in
econd-floor rooms,
orated in 1750–70.

rme
ocleziano (**E** D1)
E. De Nicola, 78
5 39 96 77 00
un 9am–7.45pm
n imagine the
nse proportions of

these Roman baths by the
size of their remains. Built
in AD 298–306, the baths
now house one section of
the National Roman
Museum (antiquities of
various baths, sculptures,
monuments of the city)
and the basilica of Santa
Maria degli Angeli, by
Michelangelo (c. 1560),
situated in what was the
main hall and *tepidarium*.
★ **Palazzo Massimo**
alle Terme (**E** E2)
→ *Largo di Villa Peretti, 1*
Tel. 06 39 96 77 00
Tue–Sun 9am–7.45pm
Also part of the National
Roman Museum, the
Palazzo Massimo houses

one of the richest ancient
art collections (2nd century
BC–AD 4th century) in the
world. Sarcophagi, busts of
emperors, a stunning
collection of architectural
ornaments, frescos,
mosaics and a striking
reconstruction of the
triclinium (dining room) of
Villa Livia, built to display
the fresco (20–10 BC)
depicting the Garden of
Eden in its original setting.
★ **Santa Maria**
Maggiore (**E** D3)
→ *Piazza Sta Maria Maggiore*
Tel. 06 48 31 95
Daily 7am–7pm
The best preserved of the
city's four major early

Christian basilicas bears
traces of all the various
architectural styles used in
Rome for more than 1,000
years. Along the central
nave are 36 brightly colored
mosaic panels (5th century)
depicting scenes from the
Old Testament.
★ **San Pietro**
in Vincoli (**E** C4)
→ *Pza San Pietro in Vincoli, 4a*
Daily 8am–12.30pm, 4–7pm
The 5th-century basilica
contains a precious relic:
the chains (*vincoli*) worn
by St Peter as a prisoner in
Jerusalem. In the right-hand
nave is the mausoleum of
Pope Julius II, with
Michelangelo's *Moses*.

Map F →

4

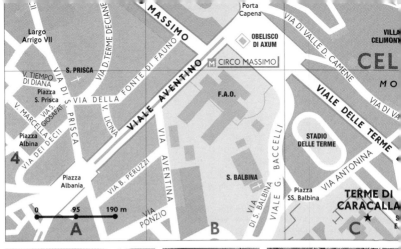

PALATINO

DOMUS AUREA

SAN CLEMENTE

★ **Campidoglio** (**F** A1)
→ *Tel. 06 67 10 24 75*
Tue-Sun 9am–8pm
(Capitoline museums)
In the 16th century, Michelangelo designed Rome's first modern piazza, in the form of a large terrace overlooking the city. At the center stands the newly restored Capitoline museums. In Palazzo dei Conservatori and Palazzo Nuovo are canvases by the Italian masters (14th–18th century), emperors' busts, the famous 5th- or 6th-century BC statue of the Capitoline Wolf and, in the courtyard, the head and hand of the huge statue of

Constantine. Entry is permitted to the ancient foundations on which the Capitol palace was founded.
★ **Foro Romano** (**F** B1)
→ *Access Via dei Fori Imperiali / Via Sacra*
Daily 9am to sunset
For an enchanting walk around the heart of ancient Rome. The forum – political, religious and commercial center of the Republic (6 BC–AD 1) – revolved around the *comitium* (where people came to hear officials speak); the *curia* (seat of the Senate); the covered basilicas (legal, political and economic affairs) and places of

worship (temples of Saturn, the Dioscuri and Vesta). During the Empire it was full of triumphal arches, built to honor the emperors.
★ **Fori Imperiali** (**F** B1)
→ *Via IV Novembre, 94*
Tel. 06 69 78 05 32
Tue-Sun 9am–4.30pm
(6.30pm in summer). Reserve ahead for guided tours
All that remains of the Imperial Fori, built during the Roman Empire, are the Collona di Traiano (Trajan's column), a superb 130-ft-high column depicting the Romans' victories over the Dacians; the Mercato de Traiano (AD 107–113), the largest and best preserved

of all the marketplaces and Augustus's forum
★ **Palatino** (**F** B2)
→ *Via di San Gregorio/ Via Sacra. Tel. 06 699 0⸱*
Daily 9am to sunset. Res⸱ ahead for guided tours
Palatine hill is one of R most magical places. Augustus was the first make the hill his home the Palatine became t residential district of th Roman ruling class. It ⸱ now covered with ruin⸱ imperial palaces abov⸱ Roman forum. Don't m the fountain of Domus Flavia; the crytoporticc tunnel link to the Dom Aurea); Domus August⸱

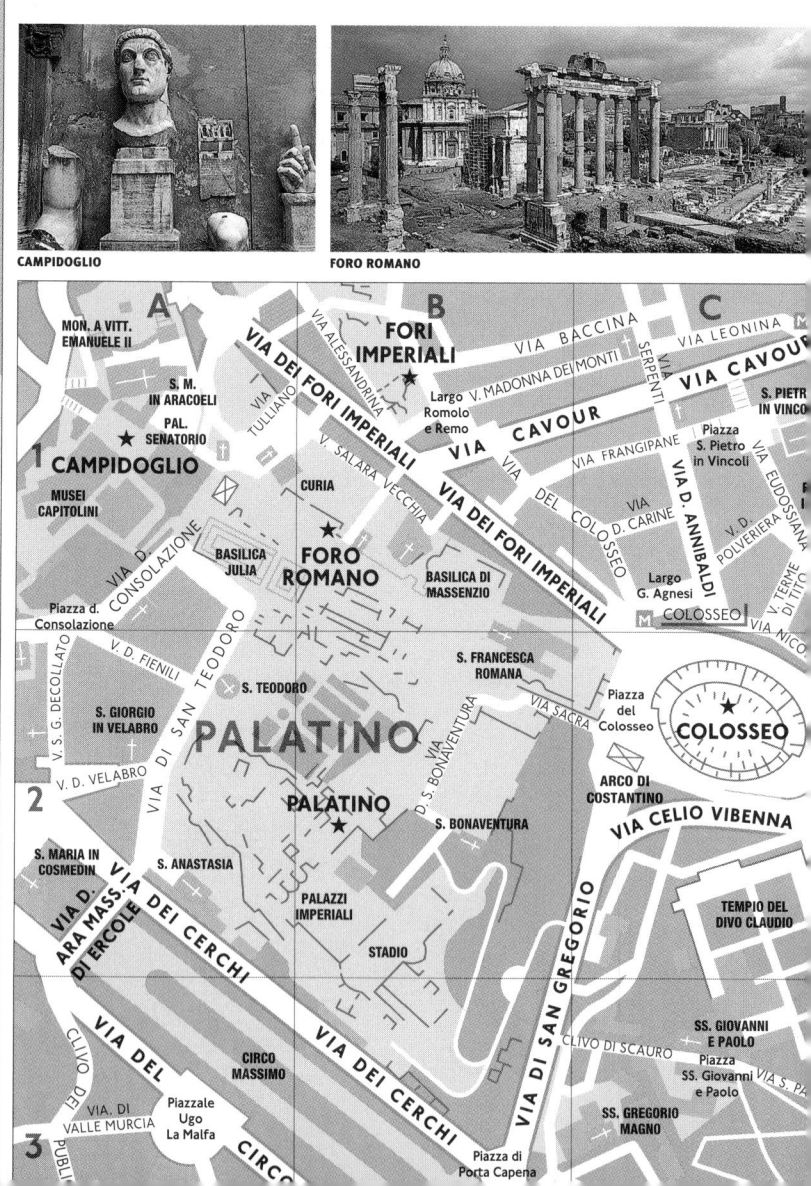

CAMPIDOGLIO

FORO ROMANO

MON. A VITT. EMANUELE II

S. M. IN ARACOELI

★ PAL. SENATORIO

CAMPIDOGLIO

MUSEI CAPITOLINI

VIA D. CONSOLAZIONE

Piazza d. Consolazione

V. D. FIENILI

V. S. G. DECOLLATO

S. GIORGIO IN VELABRO

V. D. VELABRO

VIA DI SAN TEODORO

S. TEODORO

PALATINO

PALATINO ★

S. MARIA IN COSMEDIN

VIA D. ARA MASS.

VIA DEI CERCHI

VIA D. DI ERCOLE

S. ANASTASIA

PALAZZI IMPERIALI

STADIO

CLIVO DEI PUBLI

VIA DEL

VIA. DI VALLE MURCIA

Piazzale Ugo La Malfa

CIRCO MASSIMO

VIA DEI CERCHI

CIRCO

FORI IMPERIALI ★

VIA ALESANDRINA

VIA DEI FORI IMPERIALI

Largo Romolo e Remo

V. MADONNA DEI MONTI

VIA TULLIANO

V. SALARA VECCHIA

CURIA

BASILICA JULIA

★ **FORO ROMANO**

BASILICA DI MASSENZIO

VIA DEI FORI IMPERIALI

VIA DEL COLOSSEO

VIA D. CARINE

S. FRANCESCA ROMANA

VIA SACRA

VIA D. S. BONAVENTURA

S. BONAVENTURA

Piazza del Colosseo

ARCO DI COSTANTINO

VIA DI SAN GREGORIO

CLIVO DI SCAURO

Piazza di Porta Capena

VIA BACCINA

VIA SERPENTI

VIA LEONINA

VIA CAVOUR

VIA MADONNA DEI MONTI

VIA CAVOUR

VIA FRANGIPANE

S. PIETR IN VINCO

Piazza S. Pietro in Vincoli

VIA EUDOSSIANA

VIA D. ANNIBALDI

Largo G. Agnesi

COLOSSEO

V. D. POLVERIERA

V. TERME DI TITO

VIA NICO

★ **COLOSSEO**

VIA CELIO VIBENNA

TEMPIO DEL DIVO CLAUDIO

SS. GIOVANNI E PAOLO

Piazza SS. Giovanni VIA S. PA e Paolo

SS. GREGORIO MAGNO

From the superb Piazza del Campidoglio (Capitol) by Michelangelo, take in the breathtaking view of the Foro Romano (Roman forum) – twelve centuries at one glance. In the distance is the silhouette of the Coliseum. Looming over the Forum is the Palatine hill, best seen in the late afternoon when the sun catches the ruins of the imperial palaces. Behind the Palatino is Monte Celio (the Coelian hill), where fortified churches and villas have been converted to museums and amazing gardens. To the south are the Terme di Caracalla, which had a capacity of nearly 1,600 and were the work of just one emperor, Caracalla (AD 188–217). All in all, a fascinating trip through time.

I BUONI AMICI

CANNAVOTA

RESTAURANTS

Isidoro (F D2)
→ Via San Giovanni in Laterano, 59a
Tel. 06 700 82 66 Daily 12.30–3pm, 7.30–11pm (closed Sat lunch)
This restaurant first opened over 50 years ago and is still renowned for its superb range of risotti (with strawberries or nettles) and pasta dishes such as ravioli al burro e salvia (with sage and butter). For secondi: roast veal, fish and liver. For dessert try scamorza e miele (cheese and honey). À la carte €15–20.

I Buoni Amici (F F2)
→ Via Aleardo Aleardi, 4/8
Tel. 06 70 49 19 93
Mon-Sat 12.30–3pm, 7.30–11pm
The cheerful ambience generated by the boisterous locals, along with the generous portions, makes this place feel like the local canteen. Michele is at the stove preparing simple, traditional Roman fare, while his brother, Nino, oversees the dining room. Reservations necessary. À la carte €20.

Da Romolo e Remo (F E4)
→ Via Pannonia, 22–26
Tel. 06 77 20 81 87

Tue-Sun noon–3pm, 7–11pm
Two large dining rooms, an understated, traditional interior and large tables to share – more often than not ensuring an animated evening! But the restaurant's strong point is its endless menu: 38 types of pizza, 44 primi, 36 secondi and 22 desserts! Fish and meat menu from €20–25.

Cannavota (F F3)
→ Piazza San Giovanni in Laterano, 20
Tel. 06 77 20 50 07 Thu-Tue 12.30–3pm, 7.30–11pm
A large, sunny room with a high ceiling and slightly rustic-style decor. On the walls hang photos of the celebrities who have eaten here since 1962. There's a good choice of antipasti, tasty cannelloni alla Canova (mushroom and scallops) and marvelous seafood main dishes. Fast, friendly service and generous servings. À la carte €25. Reservations essential.

Il Tempio di Iside (F E2)
→ Via Pietro Verri, 11
Tel. 06 700 47 41
Mon-Sat noon–2.30pm, 8–11.30pm
Gourmet seafood restaurant with some Sardinian dishes. Antipasti include good

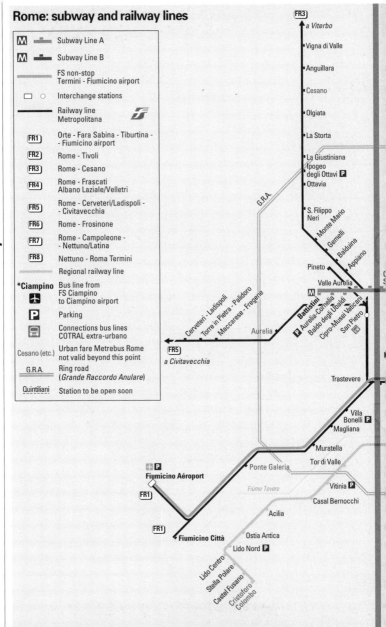

AIRPORTS

Rome has two international airports:

Aeroporto Leonardo da Vinci–Fiumicino
Seventeen miles (28 km) to the southwest of the city.

Aeroporto G.B. Pastine–Ciampino
Nine miles (18 km) to the south-east. Charter and low-cost flights only.

Information
→ Tel. 06 659 51
www.adr.it

Tourist information
There's an ATP (Azienda di Promozione Turistica) counter in both airports.

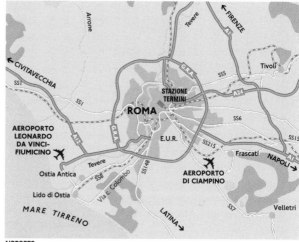

AIRPORTS

Except otherwise stated, prices given are per night, for a double room with private bathroom, in low and high season, inclusive of taxes and with breakfast. The range of Bed & Breakfasts, pensioni and residenza in central Rome is vast but rates are still high.
• Many places offer lower rates out of season (Nov-Jan, July-Aug). Better deals are to be had outside of the historic center, where, for the same price, you will find a better range of services and superior quality accommodation.
• Air conditioning is not standard in all rooms – ask the hotel when booking.

Convents
Pastoral Information Center
→ Via Santa Giovanna d'Arco, 10
Tel. 06 68 80 38 15
Fax 06 68 323 24 Mon-Fri 10am–12.30pm, 2.30–5pm
centpastrome@hotmail.com

Help in finding a room in a convent or a pensione. There is usually a curfew sometime between 10–11pm. Budget €35–40 per person in twin rooms plus contribution toward daily costs. Send your request via fax or email. They also provide seats for the public audiences of the Holy Father.

Bed & Breakfast
The APT (Azienda di Promozione Turistica) information kiosks carry lists of B&Bs. €60–100 per person per night.

Bed & Breakfast a Roma
→ Tel. 06 614 83 88
Mon 3–6pm; Tue-Fri 10am–1pm, 3–6pm
www.bb-roma.it
Provides a list of addresses throughout the city, suitable for all budgets.
And
www.italianbandb.com
www.romebandb.com
www.guestinitaly.com

Renting a flat
An economic and comfortable solution for a short or long stay. From studios to houses.
www.romesweethome.it

Less than €100

Pensione di Rienzo (E E3)
→ Via Principe Amedeo, 79a
Tel. 06 446 71 31
Near to Termini station, simply decorated, clean rooms lead onto a flowered interior courtyard. Warm welcome. €40–75 (without breakfast).

Maison de Marta (B F2)
→ Via Tacito, 41
Tel. 06 68 89 29 92
www.martaguesthouse.com
Six bedrooms with character, in a late 18th-century palace behind Castle Sant'Angelo. €65–125 (without breakfast).

Pensione Panda (D C4)
→ Via della Croce, 35

Tel. 06 678 01 79
www.hotelpanda.it
A family guest house on two floors of a 17th-century building, situated 50 yards from the Piazza di Spagna. The 28 rooms are clean and simply decorated. €98 (without breakfast).

Best Bed and Breakfast (B D1)
→ Via degli Scipioni, 135
Tel. 06 32 65 27 58
www.bestbb.it
Behind the Vatican, four beautifully decorate bedrooms in a vast apartment. €80–140.

Hotel Perugia (F C1)
→ Via del Colosseo, 7
Tel. 06 679 72 00
www.hperugia.it
Spotless, very reasonably priced hotel, particularly considering its proximity to the Coliseum. €90–135. Discounts if you stay at least three nights.

Grifo (E C3)
→ Via del Boschetto, 144

MPERIALI

COLOSSEO

← Map E

D VIA GIOVANNI Piazza
S. Martino
ai Monti

VIA IN SELCI

E LANZA Largo VIA D. STATUTO
Brancaccio

V.P. ROSSI

Piazza Vittorio
Emanuele II

F VIA RICASOLI

SQUILINO

PALAZZO
BRANCACCIO

VITTORIO EMANUELE Ⓜ

-LLE SETTE SALE VIALE DEL MONTE OPPIO

VIALE CESARE CERADINI

PARCO DI
TRAIANO

V. DELLE TERME
DI TRAIANO

VIA LEOPARDI

1

VIA MERULANA

VIA BUONARROTI

VIA EMANUELE FILIBERTO

V. FOSCOLO

V. CAIROLI

ONTE ESQUILINO

DEL MONTE ESQUILINO VIA D. ORTI DI MECENATE

CISTERNA
DELLE
SETTE SALE

VIA MECENATE

TEATRO
BRANCACCIO

VIA MACHIAVELLI

VIA GIUSTI

Piazza
Dante

VIA TASSO

TERME
DI TRAIANO

VIALE FORTUNATO MIZZI

VIA C. POLIZIANO

VIA A. BOTTA

VIA ALFIERI

VIA ARIOSTO

PARCO
OPPIO

VIA DOMUS AUREA

P. DOMUS
AUREA

VIA RUGGERO BONGHI

S. ANNA

VIA GALILEI

MANZONI Ⓜ

VIA LABICANA

VIA L. MURATORI

Piazza
Iside

VIA P. VILLARI

VIALE A. MANZONI

2

VIA TASSO

DI SAN GIOVANNI IN LATERANO

STILIA DEI SS.

CAPO

M.

ANNIA

S. CLEMENTE ★

Piazza
S. Clemente

VIA QUATTRO

D'AFRICA

VIA CELIMONTANA

SS. QUATTRO
CORONATI

V. DEI QUERCETI

AURELIO

VIA P. VERRI

VIA LABICANA

VIA DI SAN GIOVANNI IN LATERANO

SS. MARCELLINO
E PIETRO

➕

VIA DEI SS. QUATTRO

VIA MERULANA

S. ANTONIO
DA PADOVA

V.A. ALEARDI

VIA M. BOIARDO

MUSEO D.
LOTTA DI
LIBERAZIONE

VIA D.
FONTANA

Piazza
Celimontana

➕

VIA ANNIA

S. STEFANO ROTONDO

Piazza
S. Giovanni
in Laterano

S. GIOVANNI
IN LATERANO

VIA DI

OSPEDALE
S. GIOVANNI

➕

SANATORIO
UMBERTO I

➕

ADAM

BATTISTERO
LATERANENSE

PALAZZO
LATERANENSE

★

S. GIOVANNI

3

E ROCK CAFE   MERCATO DI VIA SANNIO   SUGUNARU

salmon carpaccio, smoked tuna and octopus salad. For *primi*: linguine with shrimp, crawfish and clams or gnocchetti with shrimp and asparagus tips. Fish dishes: turbot, sea bream with artichokes and potatoes. Set menu from €30.

Ai Tre Scalini (F D2)
→ *Via dei S.S. Quattro, 30*
Tel. 06 709 63 09
Tue-Sat noon–4pm,
6.30–midnight
Just a couple of paces from the Coliseum, Ai Tre Scalini offers high-quality Roman cuisine based on traditional recipes, tweaked with imagination and talent: *spaghetti di mare 'ai tre scalini'* (pesto, calamari and tiger prawns); and for dessert, a delectable chocolate mousse. You can eat on the terrace or in the dining room, harmoniously designed to complement the old building. The prices are surprisingly reasonable for the area. À la carte from €35.

ICE CREAM PARLORS, CAFÉS

Il Kiosko (F D2)
→ *Parco Oppio*
In Colle Oppio park, a music booth with several

tables scattered in front, serving ice creams and cold drinks. A great place to stop for refreshment, in a magical setting with a bird's-eye view of the Coliseum.

BARS, PUBS

Shamrock (F D2)
→ *Via Capo d'Africa, 26d*
Tel. 06 700 25 83
Daily 7.30pm–2am
A traditional Irish pub: six draught beers, whiskies and cider. At the rear is a small stage featuring local musicians. Popular with students.

Kick Off (F D1)
→ *Via delle Terme di Traiano, 4a*
Tel. 06 489 043 43
Tue-Sun 8pm–2am
A former sports center clubhouse turned into an English-style pub. The walls are covered with sports oddities: original jerseys from the Roma and Lazio team players, some unusual pairs of football boots. Low ceilings, couches, tables laid out in a semicircle and cozy cubicles. Large terrace in a gloriously green setting, close to the Terme di Traiano park. Usually quiet in the

afternoons, much livelier in the evenings when 1970s and 1980s, or house music start playing. Short menu available.

Dome Rock Cafe (F F3)
→ *Via Domenico Fontana, 16–18*
Tel. 06 704 524 36 Daily 6pm–2am (3am Fri-Sat)
Situated close to the Piazza San Giovanni, this former depot has been converted into a bar. The post-industrial decor is reminiscent of New York lofts but with weird Gothic touches: stained-glass windows, chandeliers and wrought-iron furniture. It hosts regular exhibitions by young artists. Jazz is played the first three days of the week, house and pop music at the end. A wide variety of beers and 40 different whiskies are on offer. Happy hour daily until 10.30pm. Beware: the place is always packed so get there early.

Il Posto delle Fragole (F E1)
→ *Via Carlo Botta, 51*
Tel. 06 47 82 31 25
Tue-Sat 8pm–2am
A dynamic cultural center linking Scandinavia and Italy via films, video art and painting exhibitions. In the evening different types of traditional music

such as *pizzica* from the Puglia region, jazz or samba are played live. The bar also offers delectable dishes from Sweden, Denmark and elsewhere in the north.

SHOPPING

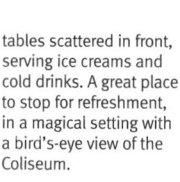

Sugunaru (F F4)
→ *Via di San Giovanni in Laterano, 206*
Tel. 06 70 49 17 19
Mon 4–8pm; Tue-Sat 10am–1pm, 4–8pm
A little boutique and workshop in one. At the old sewing machine, Marcella Manfredini creates clothes printed with asymmetric forms and unusual designs. Items also available by other designers.

Mercato di Via Sannio (F F4)
→ *Mon-Fri 8am–1pm, Sat 8am–5pm (until 6pm Nov-April)*
Backing up onto the Aurelian Wall is a type of souk, a market comprising three covered aisles and selling shoes, bags, new and second-hand clothing etc. A miniature 'Porta Portese' market, but better organized and better stocked. Enjoy haggling!

LINKS TO CITY CENTER

From Fiumicino
By train
→ Every 30 mins; journey 30 mins; one-way €9.50
The 'FS' line terminates at Rome's Termini station.
By taxi
→ Approx. €40; journey 40–45 mins
From Ciampino
By bus Cotral
→ Every 30 mins; journey 30 mins; one-way €1
To Anagnina station (line A); from there travel straight to Termini.
By taxi
→ Approx. €35–40 (30–40 mins)

TRAIN STATIONS

Stazione Centrale
Roma Termini (E F2)
The station for national and international trains.
Information
→ Tel. 892 021 freephone
www.trenitalia.it
www.romatermini.it
Other railway stations
→ Roma Tiburtina
From Tiburtina to the city center take the subway (line B) or the bus.
→ Roma Ostiense (**C** D6)
Terminus of the regional railway line; connection to Termini.
→ Roma Flaminio (**D** B3)
Terminus of the regional railway line. On line A of the subway.

Tel. 06 487 19 55
www.hotelgrifo.com
Famous for its magnificent terraces (communal or private) with views over the neighboring gardens. Immaculate, very light rooms. €90–155.

€100–140

Hotel Ivanhoe (E C3)
→ Via Urbana, 50
Tel. 06 474 31 86
www.hotelivanhoe.it
In a recessed area with palm trees and an ocher façade. The attraction of the Ivanhoe is its roof terrace and the charm of the area. Classic-style rooms with all mod-cons. €100–160.
Smeraldo (A D4)
→ Vicolo dei Chiodaroli, 9
Tel. 06 687 59 29
www.smeraldoroma.com
An 'international' hotel close to the Campo dei Fiori, with 50 pristine, well-equipped rooms (all with

air conditioning, some with a balcony). Helpful, multilingual reception staff. Terrace. From €110–140 (without breakfast).
Aventino (C D4)
→ Via di San Domenico, 10
Tel. 06 574 52 31
www.aventinohotels.com
The perfect retreat for those who need silent nights. The friendly, family-run Aventino sits in a lush green setting and has 21 light, elegantly decorated rooms. From €114–197 (without breakfast).
Pensione Barrett (A D4)
→ Largo Torre Argentina, 47
Tel. 06 686 84 81
www.pensionebarrett.com
One of the best deals to be had in central Rome. The pensione is on the second floor of an attractive palazzo overlooking, at the front, the ruins of the Area Sacra. Twenty small(ish) but impeccable rooms, well furnished (those at the

back are quieter). €110. No credit cards.
Domus Aventina (F A4)
→ Via di Santa Prisca, 11b
Tel. 06 574 61 35
www.hoteldomusaventina.it
A 17th-century façade, a vaulted entrance hall adorned with frescos, and 26 large rooms. Those with balconies or terraces overlook the garden, set between the cloister and the church of Santa Prisca. Very peaceful. €130–240.
Navona (A D3)
→ Via dei Sediari, 8
Tel. 06 686 42 03
www.hotelnavona.com
In a palazzo built on the ruins of a Roman theater. Rooms 1 to 5 are built on what was the artist's dressing rooms and room 14 is in Agrippina's former bathroom. The hotel was completely refurbished in 2004. €125–140.
Nerva (E B4)
→ Via Tor de' Conti 3

Tel. 06 678 18 35
www.hotelnerva.com
Impeccable, comfortable, modern hotel. Some of the 22 spacious and bright rooms have exposed beams or mezzanine. €130–220.
Hotel Suisse (D D4)
→ Via Gregoriana, 54
Tel. 06 678 36 49
www.hotelsuisserome.com
A couple of steps from the Piazza di Spagna. Parquet flooring, dark-wood 1930s furniture and immaculate walls, all add real character to the 12 restful bedrooms. €135–160.

€140–250

Hotel Trevi (E A2)
→ Vicolo del Babuccio, 20–21
Tel. 06 678 95 63
www.gruppotrevi.it
Situated in a small street close to the Trevi Fountain, a small hotel with a glorious flower-covered façade and

ROTONDO OSPIZIO DELLA ADDOLORATA ATENEO LATERANENSE IN LATERANO

VIA DELLA NAVICELLA

VIA DI S. ERASMO

VIA AMBA A

V. DRUSIANA

V. D. LATERAN

I O

VIA D. FERRATELLA

Piazzale Ipponio

VIA ATELIA

VIA SANNIO

Piazza di Porta Metronia

VIA IPPONIO

V. FARSALO

V. MARRUVIO

Porta Metronia

VIA TRACIA

VIA ILLIRIA

VIA SIBARI

VIA APULIA

VIA METAPONTO

VIA OLBIA

VIA LUNI

4

VIA DRUSO

CALVARELLI

MONTE

VIALE METRONIO

VIA GALLIA

VIA NORICO

VIA PANNONIA

VIA ALESIA

VIA LICIA

VIA GALLIA

V. PANDOSIA

S. SISTO VECCHIO

PARCO EGERIO

NATIVITÀ DI NOSTRO SIGNORE

Piazzale na Pompilio

D

VIA METRONIO

E

V. TAURASIA

F

IOVANNI IN LATERANO

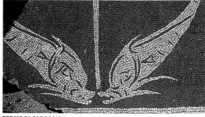

TERME DI CARACALLA

tadium; and the os in Casa di Livia.
●losseo (**F** C2)
→ *zza del Colosseo*
6 39 96 77 00
9am to sunset
most stunning Roman nitheater. In AD 80 organized 100 days lebrations to mark its ing, costing the lives 000 gladiators and animals. Built on three s, the Coliseum seated ●o spectators, all cted from the sun by ssive canvas stretched the building. Under rena is a network of els housing machinery, s and portable designs.

★ **Domus Aurea** (**F** C2)
→ *Via del Monte Oppio*
Tel. 06 39 96 77 00
Wed-Mon 9am–7.45pm
(last entry 6.45pm)
In a park that occupied a quarter of the surface area of the city, Nero built his Domus Aurea (golden villa), evidence of his megalomania. In the late 16th century, ornate 'grottos' containing magnificent frescos were unearthed, inspiring many Renaissance artists, and giving rise to the Grotesque style.

★ **San Clemente** (**F** D2)
→ *Via di San Giovanni in Laterano. Tel. 06 774 00 21*
Daily 9am (10am Sun)–
12.30pm, 3.30–6.30pm
Amazingly, you can find architecture spanning 17 centuries here! Behind the 18th-century façade is a 12th-century church. The sacristy leads down to the first basilica, dating from the 4th century, with frescos dating from the 9th, 11th and 12th centuries. At the rear of the nave, a stairway leads to a 1st-century Roman site.

★ **San Giovanni in Laterano** (**F** F3)
→ *Piazza S. Giovanni in Laterano. Tel. 06 69 88 64 33*
Daily 7am–6.30pm
The cathedral of Rome (papal seat until the 15th

century) was built on the site of a 4th-century basilica. Successive refurbishments resulted in a patchwork of architectural styles: 18th-century façade, 15th-century carved-wood ceilings and a 13th-century mosaic in the apse. The baptistery, remodeled in the 17th century, houses 4th- to 5th-century mosaics.

★ **Terme di Caracalla** (**F** C4)
→ *Viale delle Terme di Caracalla, 52*
Tel. 06 39 96 77 00
Mon 9am–2pm;
Tue-Sun 9am–7.30pm
The best preserved of all the imperial baths.

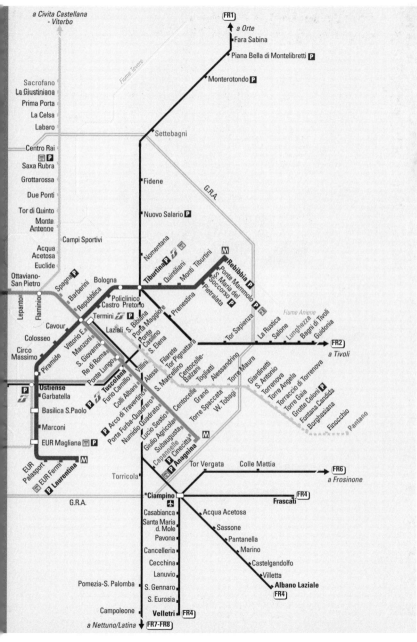

a Civita Castellana
- Viterbo

FR1
a Orte
Fara Sabina
Piana Bella di Montelibretti P
Monterotondo P

Fiume Tevere

Sacrofano
La Giustiniana
Prima Porta
La Celsa
Labaro

Settebagni

G.R.A.

Centro Rai P
Saxa Rubra
Grottarossa
Due Ponti
Tor di Quinto
Monte
Antenne
Campi Sportivi

Fidene

Nuovo Salario P

Acqua
Acetosa
Euclide
Ottaviano-
San Pietro

Nomentana

Tiburtina P

Rebibbia P
Ponte Mammolo P
S. Maria del
Soccorso P
Pietralata

Fiume Aniene

Lepanto
Flaminio
Spagna P
Barberini
Repubblica

Quintiliani
Monti Tiburtini

Bologna
Policlinico
Castro Pretorio
Termini

Prenestina

Tor Sapienza
La Rustica
Salone
Lunghezza
Bagni di Tivoli
Guidonia

FR2
a Tivoli

Cavour
Colosseo
Circo
Massimo
Piramide

Vittorio E.
Manzoni
S. Giovanni
Re di Roma
Ponte Lungo

S. Bibiana
Porta Maggiore
Ponte
Casilino
S. Elena
Laziali

Filerete
Tor Pignattara

Centocelle-
Batzani

Togliatti
Alessandrino
Torre Maura

Giardinetti
S. Antonio
Torrenova
Torre Angela
Torraccio di Torrenova
Torre Gaia
Grotte Celoni P
Fontana Candida
Borghesiana
Finocchio
Pantano

Ustiense P
Garbatella
Basilica S.Paolo
Marconi
EUR Magliana P

Tuscolana P
Furio Camillo
Colli Albani
Arco di Travertino
Porta Furba-Quadraro
Numidio Quadrato

Villini
Alessi
S. Marcellino

Centocelle
Grano
Torre Spaccata
W. Tobagi

EUR
Palasport
EUR Fermi
Laurentina P

Lucio Sestio
Giulio Agricola
Subaugusta
Capannelle
Cinecittà
Anagnina

Tor Vergata
Colle Mattia

FR6
a Frosinone

Torricola

*Ciampino

Frascati

FR4

G.R.A.

Casabianca
Santa Maria
d. Mole
Pavona
Cancelleria
Cecchina
Lanuvio
S. Gennaro
S. Eurosia

Acqua Acetosa
Sassone
Pantanella
Marino
Castelgandolfo
Villetta
Albano Laziale

FR4

Pomezia-S. Palomba

Campoleone

Velletri FR4

a Nettuno/Latina FR7-FR8

ON TWO WHEELS

Bicycle
A few cycle routes, more under construction.

Moped
Ideal for avoiding traffic jams. Crash helmets are compulsory (you will be stopped for not wearing one).

Rental
Happy Rent (off **E** C4)
→ *Via Piave, 49*
Tel. 06 42 02 06 75
Daily 9am–7pm
Moped: €50 per day.
Romarent (**A** C4)
→ *Vicolo dei Bovari, 7a*
Tel. 06 689 65 55
Daily 9am–7pm
Bicycle: €12 per day;
Moped: €50 per day.

TAXIS

Official taxis are yellow or white and carry a 'taxi' sign on the roof.

Fares
Basic charges
→ *€2.33 for the first 3 km (€4.91 from 10pm–7am; €3.36 on public hols from 7am–10pm) then €0.78 per km*

Additional charges
€1 per item of luggage; supplement if more than three passengers.

Tipping
10% of the total fare.

Radio taxis
Pronto Taxi
→ *Tel. 06 66 45*
Società la Capitale
→ *Tel. 06 49 94*
Società Cooperativa Autoradiotaxi Roma
→ *Tel. 06 35 70*

CARS

Not recommended due to the appalling traffic, car-free zones, lack of parking places and strictly enforced parking restrictions. Locals usually travel by moped.

Speed limits
Maximum speed limits are 80mph/130kmph on freeways; 55mph/90kmph on major roads; and 30mph/50kmph in built-up areas.

Street parking
Meter parking (coins or cards, available from tobacconists).
→ *€1 per hour*

Car pounds
Towed vehicles are released on payment of a heavy fine.
→ *Tel. 06 676 91 (police)*
Automobile Club Italia
→ *Tel. 116*

---

www.raphaelhotel.com
Ivy-covered façade and a huge terrace in the calm of a quiet cobbled street just behind Piazza Navona. The opulent entrance hall is full of antiques, sculpture and works by Picasso. Fabulous views of the city from the top-floor rooms, and from the rooftop restaurant, Bramante. €250–420. Breakfast €26.

LUXURY HOTELS

La Posta Vecchia
→ *Palo Laziale, Ladispoli, 18 miles from Fiumicino airport*
Tel. 069 949 501
www.lapostavecchia.com
A splendid 17th-century former post house with 15 acres of Italian gardens and overlooking the Tyrrhenian Sea, this was John Paul Getty's seaside villa before becoming a

hotel in 1990. A museum (open to guests) houses the remains of two ancient Roman villas, discovered beneath the foundations during restoration. Nineteen vast, grand bedrooms, an indoor swimming pool, a sublime restaurant – pure *dolce vita*. From €350.

es.hotel (**E** F3)
→ *Via Filippo Turati 171*
Tel. 06 444 841
www.eshotel.it
Built as a minimalist white block by hoteliers with a 'vision and a mission', the es.hotel is a marriage between contemporary design and technology. The 235 rooms are light and airy – all curves and lines – with specially made Art Deco-style furniture, but ultimately a little cold. There are magnificent views of Rome from the rooftop bar and restaurant. Rooftop

swimming pool, as well. From €600.

Hotel de Russie (**D** E4)
→ *Via Babuino, 9*
Tel. 06 32 88 81
www.rfhotels.com
Situated in the heart of Rome, the brainchild of hotelier Rocco Forte and designer Olga Polizzi is one of Rome's finest grand hotels. The hotel's restaurant and its bar, Stravinskij, are packed with Roman *conoscenti*. The vast terraced gardens are absolutely stunning. From €630.
Breakfast €26.

Majestic (**D** E4)
→ *Via Vittorio Veneto, 50*
Tel. 06 421 4 41
www.hotelmajestic.com
Subtle interplay between old and new: fresco-painted archways (Verdi room); walls lined with silk damask; antique furniture. A gem. €525–705. Breakfast €25.

PUBLIC TRANSPORTATION

Ticket sales
→ *Newsstands, train stations, subway stations, kiosks (with the ATAC logo)*
You cannot buy tickets on buses (except night buses).

Prices
Same tickets for bus, tram

and subway (see below).

BIT (Biglietto Integrato a Tempo)
→ *€1 (valid for 75 mins)*

BIG (Biglietto Integrato Giornaliero)
→ *€4 (valid for one day)*

Passes
→ *€16 (one week), €30 (one month)*

Turistic ticket
→ *€11 (three days)*

Subway (Cotral)
Two lines intersecting at Termini.
→ *Daily 5.30am–11.30pm (12.30am Sat)*
Line A (red)
Battistini–Anagnina.
Line B (blue)
Rebibbia–Laurentina.

Bus and tram (ATAC)
→ *Daily 5.30am–midnight on most lines*
Night bus 'N'
→ *Daily midnight–5.30am*
Electric bus
Serves the *centro storico* (lines 115, 116, 117, 119).
Information (E E1)
→ *Via Volturno, 59*
Tel. 800 431 784
Mon–Sat 8am–8pm

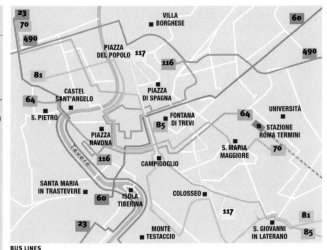

BUS LINES

a no-less attractive interior. Twenty-nine rooms with all mod-cons and classic decor. In winter breakfast is served in a vaulted room; in summer, under the plant-filled arbor. €130–340 (without breakfast).

Residenzia Zanardelli (**A** C2)
→ *Via Zanardelli, 7*
Tel. 06 68 21 13 92 (res.)
www.residenzazanardelli.com
At the top of the Piazza Navona, in a sumptuous late 18th-century baroque palace with white walls and green bronze ironwork. There are only seven rooms, with air conditioning, attractively decorated in hues of green. €145–185.

Bramante (**B** D2)
→ *Vicolo delle Palline, 24–25*
Tel. 06 687 98 81
www.hotelbramante.com
A particularly enchanting hotel. Simple, elegant decor throughout and

16 very thoughtfully decorated rooms, with masses of style. Wrought-iron bedheads, stylish furniture. Terrace. €180–240.

Hotel Celio (**F** D2)
→ *Via dei Santi Quattro, 35C*
www.hotelcelio.com Tel. 06 704 953 33
Small but opulent-looking residence, set behind the Coliseum. Plush interior with a strange but interesting mixture of styles (rococo, Art Nouveau). Mirrors, frescos or trompe-l'œil painting, and 20 quiet rooms, all designed differently. €150–290.

Campo dei Fiori (**A** C4)
→ *Via dei Biscione, 6*
Tel. 06 688 068 65
www.hotelcampodefiori.com
Rooms and apartments (for two to six people, €110–250). At the top is a fabulous terrace with panoramic views of Rome. €160–200 (with breakfast).

Teatro di Pompeo (**A** C4)
→ *Largo del Pallaro, 8*
Tel. 06 68 30 01 70
www.hotelteatrodipompeo.it
Hotel built on the foundations of consul and general Pompeii's ancient Roman theater. Twelve exquisite air-conditioned rooms, interior courtyard and a breakfast room with a view of the ruins. From 170–190 €.

Villa San Pio (**C** D5)
→ *Via di Santa Melania, 19*
www.aventinohotels.com
A country-style villa in a wilderness of greenery, with rustic-style decor in ochers and lilacs; the city could be miles away. Villa San Pio has 65 comfortable rooms, some with a view over the small lush garden where breakfast is served. €170–240.

Hotel Raphaël (**A** C3)
→ *Largo Febo, 2*
Tel. 06 68 28 31